Available
as a Group
Retreat!
See back pages
for more info.

33 Days
to
Morning
Glory

A Do-It-Yourself Retreat
in Preparation for Marian Consecration

Fr. Michael E. Gaitley, MIC

MARIAN PRESS
STOCKBRIDGE   MA 01263

PRO CHRISTO ET ECCLESIA

2014

Available from:
Marian Helpers Center
Stockbridge, MA 01263

Prayerline: 1-800-804-3823
Orderline: 1-800-462-7426
Website: www.marian.org

IMPRIMI POTEST:
Very Rev. Kazimierz Chwalek, MIC
Provincial Superior
The Blessed Virgin Mary, Mother of Mercy Province
October 7, 2011

NIHIL OBSTAT
June 24, 2012
Feast of the Nativity of Saint John the Baptist
Most Reverend Timothy A. McDonnell, D.D.,
Bishop of Springfield, Massachusetts

Library of Congress Catalog Number: 2011939271
ISBN: 978-1-596142-442
First edition (8th printing): 2014

Cover Art: "Immakulata" image © Rektoratskirche
St. Peter, Kunst und Kultur Referat

Printed in the United States of America

Acclaim for
33 Days to Morning Glory

Finally an easy way to understand and live out Marian consecration! Forget about difficult theology and out-dated language. Here, for the first time, you'll find the best Marian teachings of St. Louis de Montfort, St. Maximilian Kolbe, Blessed Mother Teresa, and Blessed John Paul II — all presented so simply and clearly that you can immediately make them your own and apply them in your daily life.

Written in Fr. Gaitley's person-to-person, conversational style, this is a book that will inspire and empower anyone to draw closer to Jesus through Mary. It will become the new manual for true devotion to Mary.

— **VINNY FLYNN**
Bestselling Author, *7 Secrets of the Eucharist*
Director, MercySong Ministries of Healing

In a day and time when the spiritual stakes have never been higher, consecration to Jesus through Mary stands as a tried and true way of attaining holiness of life. First outlined by St. Louis Grignion de Montfort, this spiritual path is an easy, sure, safe, and perfect road to travel. That is why Father Michael E. Gaitley, MIC, has done the people of God a great service with his adaptation of the 33-day preparation for the consecration.

In *33 Days to Morning Glory*, Father Gaitley highlights the teachings of St. Louis de Montfort and those of three contemporary spiritual giants as well. These saints of the Church reveal the secrets of their own pilgrimage to the Heart of Jesus through Our Lady and mentor us in our discovery of her maternal beatitude. Take this retreat and let St. Maximilian Kolbe, Blessed Teresa of Calcutta, Blessed John Paul II, and St. Louis de Montfort lead you into the mystical wonder of the Immaculate Heart. Believe me, your life will never be the same!

— **JOHNNETTE S. BENKOVIC**
Women of Grace, Founder and President
Television and Radio Host on EWTN

Father Michael Gaitley, MIC, in *33 Days to Morning Glory*, has struck gold. He mines the Biblical experience of consecration to Mary through the experiences of four giants in the field: St. Louis de Montfort, St. Maximilian Kolbe, Blessed Mother Teresa of Calcutta, and Blessed John Paul II.

Father Gaitley has an uncanny ability to cull and explain clearly the essence of each one's contribution to the field of Marian consecration: St. Louis de Montfort's passionate insistence on the totality of the gift of self; St. Maximilian Kolbe's mystical intuition about the interior union of Mary and the Holy Spirit in the life of a consecrant; Blessed Mother Teresa's experience of Mary drawing us into her heart, where Jesus keeps repeating "I thirst"; and Blessed John Paul II's understanding that consecration to Mary brings us to the source of merciful love — the Divine Mercy poised to transform the world.

I compliment Fr. Gaitley profusely for the extraordinary way in which he treats the subject of consecration — with a concrete anticipation of peoples' questions before they are even posed. I have been giving Marian talks for decades, and I have never quite read any with the particular style that God gifts Fr. Gaitley to use. Congratulations, Father. Gold, indeed!

— **FR. JAMES McCURRY, OFM CONV.**
Minister Provincial, St. Anthony of Padua Province

33 Days to Morning Glory will deepen the understanding of Marian consecration for both those who desire to make the consecration for the first time and those who have already made it. Father Michael Gaitley, MIC, brings the Marian thought of four spiritual giants together into one powerful retreat. A prayerful reading of this book will not only increase one's knowledge of Marian consecration but lead one to a closer union with Our Blessed Mother.

— **MOTHER ASSUMPTA LONG, OP**
Prioress General, Dominican Sisters of Mary,
Mother of the Eucharist

To my community,

The Marians of the Immaculate Conception
and all our lay staff and Marian Helpers.

May we love the Immaculata even more.

Everyone should have a genuine
devotion to [Mary] and entrust his
life to her motherly care.

— *Vatican II*

Contents

In Gratitude

About three weeks ago, I gave a spiritual talk to some of the new men in my religious community, the Marians of the Immaculate Conception. I spoke about our charism, mission, and identity and explained that as a particularly active community, our task is to spend ourselves in apostolic labor for the sake of Christ and the Church. Then I asked them, "And where should our zeal for this task come from?" One of them answered, "From our love for Jesus." Of course, he was absolutely right, but there's more to it. I explained, "As Marians of the Immaculate Conception, a prime source of our energy and zeal should also be a great love for Mary Immaculate." Next, I made a confession. I said, "Guys, please pray for me. I'm telling you this, but I myself need to grow here. I have a deep love for Jesus, and I'm sure Mary has a lot to do with this, but I need a jumpstart in my devotion to her."

I mention this story because these new Marian vocations, out of their deep love for Mary, have been praying for me. I believe this because, less than a month after asking for their prayers, I'm writing this book. I can't explain it except to say that I woke up one morning a week ago with the idea for this entire book in my mind and heart. Providentially, this happened right before a week of vacation, so I've been writing, non-stop, ever since.

What's most amazing to me in all this is that while it took me 10 years to finish writing my last book, *Consoling the Heart of Jesus*, in less than a week, this one's already halfway done. So, I owe many thanks to the new Marian men. Even though their prayers ruined my vacation, I'm happy because my smoldering zeal for Mary is being rekindled. My hope and prayer is that this book, written in haste but with care, will fire up other tepid souls to a greater love for Mary.

Before signing off, I'd like to thank the other people whose prayers and encouragement are helping me with this project, especially Mary Immaculate, Sr. Bernadette Marie Allain-Dupre, FM, Fr. Gregory Staab, OMV, and Erin Flynn. Also, special thanks to those who have agreed to proofread the text, particularly to Sarah Chichester, who has already provided many helpful comments and suggestions. Finally, I'm grateful to

Fr. Angelo Casimiro, MIC, and Curtis Bohner for helping design the cover, Kathy Szpak who will be laying out the pages, and to the Marian editorial team who will be making the edits: David Came and Andy Leeco. For the opportunity to work on and publish this retreat, I thank my religious family, the Congregation of Marian Fathers of the Immaculate Conception. Finally, my deepest gratitude goes to God for his many mercies, one of the greatest of which is our Immaculate Mother.

Fr. Michael E. Gaitley, MIC, STL
National Shrine of The Divine Mercy
Stockbridge, Massachusetts
July 26, 2011
Memorial of Sts. Joachim and Anne
(Parents of Mary)

Acknowledgements

Permission is gratefully acknowledged to cite from the following works:

Excerpts from *Aim Higher!: Spiritual and Marian Reflections of St. Maximilian Kolbe*. Translated by Dominic Wisz, OFM Conv. © 2007 Franciscan Marytown Press, Libertyville, IL.

Excerpts from *Immaculate Conception and the Holy Spirit* by H.M. Manteau-Bonamy, OP. Translated by Richard Arnandez, FSC. © 1977 Franciscan Marytown Press, Libertyville, IL.

Excerpts from *The Kolbe Reader*. Edited by Anselm W. Romb, OFM Conv. © 1987 Franciscan Marytown Press, Libertyville, IL.

Excerpts from *True Devotion to Mary* by St. Louis de Montfort. Translated by Frederick W. Faber. © 1985 TAN Books, Rockford, IL.

Mother Teresa's letter to the Missionaries of Charity family, 25th March 1993 © 2011 Missionaries of Charity Sisters, c/o Mother Teresa Center. Used with permission

Special thanks to Michael Collopy for permission to reproduce the image of Christ crucified on the inside front cover.

INTRODUCTION
Why I Wrote This Book, and How It Works

I wrote this book for one main reason: Total Consecration to Jesus through Mary (Marian consecration) truly is "the surest, easiest, shortest, and the most perfect means"[1] to becoming a saint, and there should be an *easy* and *updated* way to dive in to such a blessing.

N *O EASY WAY … 'TIL NOW.* I ran into a problem when I was writing my other do-it-yourself retreat, *Consoling the Heart of Jesus.* In that book, I spoke about how awesome, amazing, and life-changing total consecration to Jesus through Mary is, but I didn't have time to explain it fully. So, I recommended that people read St. Louis de Montfort's classic book on Marian consecration, *True Devotion to Mary.*

In *True Devotion,* de Montfort lays out a course of preparation for Marian consecration that lasts 33 days. Problem is, it's not so easy to follow the format as laid out in the book itself. (The prayers are on different pages, you have to hunt them down, flip back and forth, etc.) To solve this problem, the de Montfort Fathers published a smaller book called *Preparation for Total Consecration.* That book gathered all the prayers together and made it easier to follow de Montfort's 33 days, but there was still a problem for me.

De Montfort's 33-day preparation is loaded with litanies and prayers but lean on information about consecration. Years ago, when I first began his preparation format, I clearly remember the impression it made on me: "What have I gotten myself into?!" It seemed I'd begun a 33-day prayer marathon, and I wondered if I'd be able to persevere to the end. Eventually, I resigned myself to the idea that to gain the crown of Marian consecration, I'd just have to "pay my dues" by reciting the long list of prayers that grew each week. Don't get me wrong, it's fitting that we make some kind of sacrifice in order to receive a gift as great as Marian consecration. Moreover, I don't mean to disparage vocal prayer, which has immense value and is an "essential element of the Christian life."[2] It's just that I personally find more spiritual fruit not in reciting long prayers but in *pondering in my heart inspiring teachings on Marian consecration*. I've learned there are not a few others who feel the same way, and I don't want them to miss out on such a treasure as Marian consecration because of so many lengthy prayers.

So, I wrote this book. I did so with the belief that a preparation for Marian consecration (or a preparation for renewing one's consecration) doesn't have to be a prayer marathon. Rather, it can be a less daunting experience of spiritual reading and prayerful pondering. Of course, there are those who may find more spiritual nourishment in the original, 33-day preparation, and that's great. But I wanted to provide an alternative for those who, like me, sometimes struggle with saying so many long prayers. Also, I wanted to provide for everyone — litany lovers included — an updated version of St. Louis's original 33-day preparation that would include new riches from contemporary sources, a Marian consecration for the Third Millennium.

*N*O UPDATED WAY ... 'TIL NOW. In *Consoling the Heart of Jesus*, I made an amazingly bold claim. I said one could get all the graces of a 30-day Ignatian retreat not in 30 days but in just one weekend. In being so bold, I took my cue from Venerable Fr. Pio Bruno Lanteri (1759-1826), who claimed that someone could have everything he needs to become "a great saint" not in 30 days but in just 8 days. Why did Lanteri believe his retreats could be shorter than yet just as effective as 30-day retreats? Because he gave them with a special emphasis, what I call his "secret weapons": Divine Mercy and Mary. And why did I believe my retreat could be even shorter than Lanteri's? Because Lanteri died more than 180 years ago, and since his death there's been even greater insight into his secret weapons, making them even more powerful. With these more powerful weapons, I concluded that we could have even more effective retreats, even in a weekend.

So, in *Consoling the Heart of Jesus*, I spent most of the pages unpacking the rich, new insights that have to do with one of Lanteri's secret weapons: Divine Mercy. Thus, I covered a lot of material from two of the great, contemporary Mercy Saints: Thérèse of Lisieux and Maria Faustina Kowalska. Unfortunately, I didn't have as much time then to dwell on the rich, new insights concerning Marian consecration. I touched on those insights but couldn't go into great depth. Fortunately, that's what we get to do here.

In the pages that follow, we'll be hearing not only from the first great apostle of Marian consecration, St. Louis de Montfort, but also from other Marian giants who came after him. In doing this, we're simply following de Montfort's own example. In his day, he gathered and synthesized the teachings of the best experts in Marian spirituality. Were he alive today, there's no doubt he would present the teachings of our contemporary "Marian experts."

Who are the contemporary Marian experts? There are plenty of them, but I've chosen for our reflection "the big three." Specifically, I've picked the top three Marian saints who have most dramatically added to the beauty and richness of consecration spirituality. They are St. Maximillian Kolbe, Blessed Mother Teresa of Calcutta, and Blessed John Paul II. When we add St. Louis de Montfort to this mix, we've got a grand total of four Marian giants who will help lead us through a power-packed and updated form of Marian consecration.

*H*OW THE RETREAT WORKS. Every week of this four-week retreat (plus five days for review), we'll read about how one of our four giants of Marian consecration lived out his or her consecration to Jesus through Mary. The goal will be not just to read about them and their teaching but, like Mary, *to ponder their message in our hearts*. So, for 33 days, we won't be going through a long list of prayers. Rather, we'll do our best to spend all day, each day, pondering the day's teaching. (Or, if we do our reading in the evenings, we can spend the day pondering the previous day's teaching.) As we know from Sacred Scripture, this heart-pondering attitude is specifically Marian (see Luke 2:19, 51), and it's something we can do no matter how busy we are. Moreover, I've included a short prayer to go with each day's reading to help us ponder the day's lesson. And because our goal during these 33 days is to remain in an atmosphere of heart-pondering prayer, I've called this time not just a preparation but a *retreat*.

Of course, 33 days is a long time to be on retreat, and it just might happen that, despite our good intentions and best efforts, we'll miss a day (or days) of the readings and prayers. If this happens, we need not get discouraged, and we surely shouldn't quit! Instead, I suggest that we simply read the text for the days we missed as soon as we can and keep going with the retreat. The Lord knows what's in our hearts, and if our desire truly is to make the consecration, we shouldn't let any temptations stop us. Believe me, it's very likely that we'll face temptations to cancel our preparation. But let's not give in. Let's do our best to be faithful to the readings and the prayerful pondering for each day. If we falter because of negligence, let's tell the Lord we're sorry, trust in his mercy, make up the missed readings, and keep going.

The reason I suggest that we make up any missed readings has to do with the structure of the retreat: Each day's teaching builds on the next, and all the parts converge at the end to give a complete picture of Marian consecration. So, we surely wouldn't want to skip an essential part. Moreover, because this retreat is so structured, it may be helpful at the outset to briefly consider a breakdown of the four full weeks of the retreat, keeping in mind that the last five days are reserved for review:

| Week 1 – St. Louis de Montfort |
| Week 2 – St. Maximillian Kolbe |
| Week 3 – Blessed Mother Teresa |
| Week 4 – Blessed John Paul II* |

---

* Again, five days remain after the fourth week. The first four of these days (29-32) are dedicated, in turn, to a review of each one of the weeks. The fifth day (day 33 of the preparation) is reserved for reviewing the prayer of consecration that will be recited the following day, the Marian Feast, the "34th" day.

Now, before we begin the retreat itself, I thought I'd include an introduction to Marian consecration. This introduction is not part of the 33 days of preparation. Instead, it's a kind of preparation for the preparation. And this is a good thing, because while the introduction can be read at any time, I recommend doing the retreat itself during one of several specific times. In other words, I suggest that we follow St. Louis's advice to schedule the 33 days of preparation so they will end on the vigil of a Marian feast day. To help us figure out when we might want to begin, here's a chart that breaks down the starting dates and feasts:

START OF THE 33 DAYS	MARIAN FEAST	CONSECRATION/ FEAST DAY
January 9	Our Lady of Lourdes	February 11
February 20*	The Annunciation	March 25
April 10	Our Lady of Fatima	May 13
April 28	The Visitation	May 31
Varies	Immaculate Heart	Saturday after Corpus Christi
June 13	Our Lady of Mt. Carmel	July 16
July 13	The Assumption	August 15
July 20	Queenship of Mary	August 22
August 6	Nativity of Mary	September 8
August 10	Holy Name of Mary	September 12
August 13	Our Lady of Sorrows	September 15
September 4	Our Lady of the Rosary	October 7
October 19	Presentation of Mary	November 21
November 5	Immaculate Conception	December 8
November 9	Our Lady of Guadalupe	December 12
November 29	Mother of God	January 1
December 31	Presentation of the Lord	February 2

* During a leap year, when February has 29 days, the starting date is February 21.

So, with St. Louis, I highly recommend that you wait to begin the retreat on one of the above starting dates. Having said this, I should add that there's never a bad time or a wrong time to prepare for consecration. This is just the ideal. If you do decide to wait for one of the starting dates, you don't have to wait to read the following introduction. In fact, you can start reading it right now.

Actually, before you begin the introduction, here's one more thing you might want to consider: making a group retreat. While it's customary to make retreats on one's own, many people find small-group formats to be particularly effective. If you're interested in this option, see the information pages at the end of this book.

Introduction to Marian Consecration

*W*HY *"MORNING GLORY"?* When you first saw this book, you may have wondered, "Why is it called *33 Days to Morning Glory?*" The "33 days" part should now be clear — it refers to the days of preparation — but maybe the "morning glory" part isn't so clear. I chose this part of the title because I think it best captures what Marian consecration is all about: A new way of life in Christ. The act of consecrating oneself to Jesus through Mary marks the beginning of a gloriously new day, a new dawn, a brand new morning in one's spiritual journey. It's a fresh start, and it changes everything.

I had the experience of a gloriously new morning in my own spiritual journey when I consecrated myself to Mary* for the first time on December 8, 1995. It was the end of the first

---

* Sometimes I will refer in this book to Marian consecration as a consecration "to Jesus through Mary;" at other times, I will refer to it simply as a consecration "to Mary." The two expressions have the same meaning. After all, Mary's whole purpose and mission is to bring souls into union with her divine Son, Jesus. She's not in competition with him. So, if I say "consecration *to Mary*," its full meaning is "to Jesus through Mary." In fact, any "to Mary" expression used in this book should be taken as "to Mary ... for the sake of Christ, for the sake of God, for the sake of the Trinity." Here on out, I'm going to presuppose this because it would be too repetitive to explain it every time.

semester of my freshman year in college. Earlier that semester, a friend had given me a copy of St. Louis de Montfort's book, *True Devotion to Mary*. When I saw the words on the back cover, declaring that it presents a "short, easy, secure, and perfect" way to become a saint, I was sold. I thought to myself, "Hey, this is the kind of way I need!" So, despite having a pile of homework, I started reading. Before I was even halfway through the book, I stopped, set it down, and resolutely decided, "I will do this consecration." Afterward, I picked the next available Marian feast, ran the 33-day prayer marathon, and made the consecration with great fervor. That day totally changed my life. I look back on it now, and I can truly say that everything changed. Everything opened up. It was a gloriously new morning in my walk with Christ, now with Mary.

Blessed John Paul II describes consecration to Mary as having had a similar effect on him. He even says that his reading of de Montfort's book was a "turning point" in his life.[3] In fact, his consecration to Jesus through Mary was so important to him that he adopted as his papal motto de Montfort's own words that summarize total consecration to Jesus through Mary, "*Totus Tuus*," ("Totally Yours"). Also, it's reported that the Pope recited the long version of de Montfort's consecration prayer every day.

I've met many people who have consecrated themselves to Mary, and they completely relate to the Pope's words about how it's a turning point in one's life — or, as I put it, "a gloriously new morning" in one's spiritual journey. It truly does make a difference. It truly is "the surest, easiest, shortest, and the most perfect means" to becoming a saint, which brings me to another reason why I chose to include "Morning Glory" in the title.

*T*HE DAWN OF GLORIOUSLY NEW SAINTS. As I mentioned in the introduction to *Consoling the Heart of Jesus*, St. Louis de Montfort predicted a couple of interesting things about his book, *True Devotion to Mary*. First, he said that after his death, angry demons would come to hide the unpublished manuscript so no one could ever read it — and, in fact, the manuscript was lost for more than a century after his death. The saint wrote:

I clearly see that raging beasts shall come in fury to
tear with their diabolical teeth this little writing ... or
at least to smother it in the darkness and silence of a
coffer, that it may not appear.[4]

De Montfort went on to say that his manuscript would
eventually be discovered and published and that its Marian
spirituality would help form some of the greatest saints in the
history of the Church. Moreover, his prediction about these
saints wasn't that they would be just a few people. Rather, he
hoped there'd be a whole army of these greatest of saints:

This very foresight [about the beasts coming for the
manuscript] encourages me, and makes me hope for
great success, that is to say, for a great squadron of
brave and valiant soldiers of Jesus and Mary, of both
sexes, to combat the world, the devil, and corrupted
nature, in those more than ever perilous times which
are about to come.[5]

In this passage, de Montfort describes the times that
would come as "more than ever perilous." I don't think anyone
would argue with me that we live in perilous times. In fact, in
many ways, our time truly is marked by unprecedented evil.
But don't worry, because here's some good news: In times of
unprecedented evil, God wants to give unprecedented grace.
For, as St. Paul wrote, "Where sin abounds grace abounds all
the more" (Rom 5:20). And one of the ways God gives his
superabundant grace in our time is by raising up some of the
greatest saints ever. Saint Louis describes these saints as follows:

The Most High with His holy Mother has to form for
Himself great saints who shall surpass most of the
other saints in sanctity as much as the cedars of
Lebanon outgrow little shrubs.[6]

How can this be? The saints who have come before us
surely are impressive. Moreover, the virtue and holiness of people

in our day — present company included — isn't exactly stellar. Yet, that's the amazing point. God wants to form saints from the little souls. He wants to form saints according to the pattern of the Immaculate Conception of Mary. Look at it this way: The Immaculate Conception of Mary, the grace whereby she was conceived without the stain of original sin, is an incredible gift of mercy. What's particularly remarkable is that *Mary did nothing to deserve or merit this grace*. It was a total gift — won by the merits of her Son. Mary wasn't an embryo in the womb of her mother, St. Anne, praying the Rosary to merit this gift. Rather, she received it at the very moment of her conception, the very moment she came into being. So, she did absolutely nothing to deserve it. It was God's own initiative to give this totally free and wonderful gift.

So with us. God is offering the people of our time a powerful and effective way to become great saints, and it's not because we're so good. Rather, it's because our times are so perilous, and God wants his mercy to triumph through Mary. So, he gives us poor, sinful souls an amazing gift — what St. Louis calls a little known "secret":

> Poor children of Mary, your weakness is extreme, your inconstancy is great, your inward nature is very much corrupted. You are drawn (I grant it) from the same corrupt mass as all the children of Adam and Eve. Yet do not be discouraged because of that. Console yourselves and exult in having the secret which I will teach you — a secret unknown to almost all Christians, even the most devout.[7]

What is this blessed "secret"? It's the spirituality of a true devotion to Mary, a spirituality of total consecration to Jesus through Mary. It's what this retreat is all about. Before we begin, I should give a summary explanation of Marian consecration, the understanding of which will deepen over the course of our retreat.

*W*HAT IS MARIAN CONSECRATION? What follows is the overview of Marian consecration that I presented in my book, *Consoling the Heart of Jesus*. If you've already read it there, feel free to skip this section. However, it doesn't hurt to review, right?

To properly understand the essence of total consecration to Jesus through Mary, we'll first need to reflect on an important point: Jesus wants to include all of us in his work of salvation. In other words, he doesn't just redeem us and then expect us to kick back and relax. On the contrary, he puts us to work. He wants all of us to labor in his Father's vineyard in one way or another. Why he didn't just snap his fingers and so order things that everyone in the world would individually hear and understand the Gospel by some private, mystical revelation, we don't know. What we do know is that Jesus relies on others to spread his Gospel and that he commissions his disciples to preach it to all (see Mt 28:19-20). He basically says to them and to us, "Let's get to work!" Of course, that God wants to include us in his work of salvation is a great gift and glorious privilege. Truly, there's no more important work to be done.

While everyone is called to lend a hand in the great work of salvation, not everyone has the same role. For example, St. Paul says, "There are varieties of service and … there are varieties of working" (1 Cor 12:5-6). He goes on to say that God has appointed to the work of salvation "first apostles, second prophets, third teachers, then workers of miracles, then healers, helpers, administrators" (v. 28). Whoever we are, God has appointed us to a special task in his great work.

Among the various roles God has given to his children, there's one that's radically more important than all the others: the task he gave to Mary. We all know that God uniquely blessed Mary by choosing her to conceive, bear, and nurture Jesus Christ, our Savior. But do we also realize that her blessed work didn't end once Jesus left home and began his public ministry? After the three years of Mary's hidden life during Jesus' public ministry, Jesus brought her back into the picture of his work of salvation at its most crucial time, the "hour" of his Passion. At that hour, we might say he fully revealed Mary's special task — the same task she had begun some 33 years before and that she still continues.

Jesus fully revealed Mary's special task shortly before his death. It happened when he looked down from the Cross and said to Mary as she stood with the Apostle John, "Woman, behold, your son" and to John, "Behold, your mother" (Jn 19:26-27). At that moment, Jesus gave us one of his greatest gifts: his mother as our mother. Of course, Mary isn't our natural mother. She's our spiritual mother. In other words, just as it was once her task some 2,000 years ago to give birth to Christ, to feed and nurture him, and to help him grow and develop into a man, so also, from the time she first said yes to being the mother of Jesus until the end of time, Mary's task is to give spiritual birth to Christians, to feed and nurture them with grace, and to help them grow to full stature in Christ. In short, Mary's job is to help us grow in holiness. It's her mission to form us into saints.

"Now, wait just a minute," someone might say, "isn't it the job of the Holy Spirit to make us holy?" Indeed, it is. The Holy Spirit is the Sanctifier. It is he who transforms us at our Baptism from being mere creatures into members of the Body of Christ, and it is he who helps us in our ongoing transformation into Christ through continued conversion. Great. So how does Mary come into all of this?

Mary is the spouse of the Holy Spirit. At the Annunciation, the angel Gabriel declared to Mary that she would conceive and bear a son and that the Holy Spirit would overshadow her (see Lk 1:31-35). When Mary said, "Behold, I am the handmaid of the Lord; let it be to me according to your word" (Lk 1:38), we can see most clearly that she's the spouse of the Holy Spirit, for at that moment, she gave the Holy Spirit permission to conceive Christ in her womb. Thus, at that moment, the already unfathomably deep bond between Mary and the Holy Spirit that had begun (in time) at the first moment of her Immaculate Conception was revealed as nothing less than a two-become-one marital union (see Gen 2:24). As a result of that union, the Holy Spirit is pleased to work and act through his spouse, Mary, for the sanctification of the human race. Of course, he didn't have to be so united to Mary.

It was his free choice (and that of the Father and the Son), and in that choice he takes delight.

So, it's Mary's great God-given task, in union with and by the power of the Holy Spirit, to form every human being into "another Christ," that is, to unite everyone to the Body of Christ and form each person into a fully mature member of this Body.[8] Therefore, every human being is invited to rest in the womb of Mary and be transformed there, by the power of the Holy Spirit, more perfectly into Christ's own image. Yes, if we want to become more fully Christ, then we need to belong more fully to Mary. By going to her and remaining with her, we allow her to accomplish her mission in us. We allow her to form us into other Christs, into great saints. But how do we do this? How do we belong more fully to Mary and allow her to fulfill her mission in us? Simple. We say yes, just like she did.

Mary has a deep respect for human freedom. She knows from her own experience in Nazareth what a free yes to God can do (see Lk 1:38), and so she doesn't pressure us into giving her our yes. Of course, she always cares for her children, but she won't force us to enter into a deeper relationship with her. She surely invites us to such a relationship and patiently waits for us to accept her invitation, but she remains respectful. Still, if we could see how much longing hides behind her silence, we'd say yes to her if only to give her relief. In fact, saying yes to her gives her more than relief. It gives her joy. Great joy. And the more fully we say yes to Mary, the more joyful she becomes. For our yes gives her the freedom to complete her work in us, the freedom to form us into great saints. This brings us to the essence of what Marian consecration is all about.

Marian consecration basically means giving Mary our full permission (or as much permission as we can) to complete her motherly task in us, which is to form us into other Christs. Thus, by consecrating ourselves to Mary, each of us is saying to her:

> Mary, I want to be a saint. I know that you also want
> me to be a saint and that it's your God-given mission
> to form me into one. So, Mary, at this moment, on this

day, I freely choose to give you my full permission to do your work in me, with your Spouse, the Holy Spirit.

As soon as Mary hears us make such a decision, she flies to us and begins working a masterpiece of grace within our souls. She continues this work for as long as we don't deliberately choose to change our choice from a yes to a no, as long as we don't take back our permission and leave her. That being said, it's always a good idea for us to strive to deepen our "yes" to Mary. For the deeper our "yes" becomes, the more marvelously she can perform her works of grace in our souls.

One of the greatest aspects of being consecrated to Mary is that she's such a gentle mother. She makes the lessons of the Cross into something sweet, and she pours her motherly love and solace into our every wound. Going to her and giving her permission to do her job truly is the "surest, easiest, shortest and the most perfect means" to becoming a saint. What joy it is to be consecrated to Jesus through Mary!

Now we're ready to begin the retreat and learn more about this blessed "secret" and the man who so powerfully proclaims it to the world: St. Louis Marie Grignion de Montfort.

St. Louis de Montfort

This week, we'll focus on the example and words of the first great prophet of Marian consecration. We'll begin by learning about his life, and then we'll ponder the essential aspects of his Marian teaching. [Please note: We do not have space here to cover every essential element of de Montfort's teaching. Omitted elements will be covered in later weeks.]

DAY 1
The Passionate Saint of Brittany

Take a look at a map of France. Now notice something about its shape. See how one part sticks way out almost as if it were running away from the rest of the landmass, ready to dive off into the Celtic Sea? That jutting arm in the northwest of the country is called "Brittany," and that's where St. Louis de Montfort grew up.

There's something special about Brittany that seems to have had an influence on St. Louis: its Celtic roots. Brittany is considered one of the six Celtic nations, meaning that the Celtic language and culture still survive. (So, scratch that part about Brittany being ready to dive into the Celtic Sea. It's already in and swimming.) And one part of Celtic culture seems to have seeped deeply into the heart of St. Louis: the high-spiritedness of its warriors.

From ancient times, Celtic warriors have struck terror in the hearts of their enemies. If you've ever seen the movie *Braveheart*, you know what I mean. Think of the fearless figure of Sir William Wallace (played by Mel Gibson) and his crazy crew of Scottish Highlanders who take on an English enemy many times their size. This shows something of the Celtic fighting spirit, but the real life version is even more intense.

Often wearing nothing but blue battle paint, real Celtic warriors would work themselves into a blood-thirsty frenzy, rush into combat screaming their heads off, and wildly slash, bash, and slice away at their enemies with huge, two-handed swords. These fierce fighting men, despite their lack of discipline, armor, and order, were extremely effective in battle because of their unmatched passion and ferocity. Throughout history, nobody has wanted to mess with the crazy Celtic warriors.

St. Louis's dad, Jean Grignion, must have been descended from these wild-men warriors, for nobody wanted to mess with him either. In fact, he was known for having the most fiery temper in all of Brittany. As one author puts it, "He was a volcano frequently erupting."[9] St. Louis, on the other hand, was as gentle as a lamb, right? Wrong. He confessed that his temper was just as bad as his father's. But Louis channeled his fiery passion not to threats and violence but to laboring for the greater Glory of God — well, except for the time he knocked out a couple of drunks who wouldn't stop heckling him while he preached. We can get a better sense of Louis's remarkable zeal if we reflect on his short but incredibly productive priestly life.

When he died in 1716, St. Louis was just 43 years old, having been a priest for only 16 years. Tireless labors to bring souls to Jesus through Mary, especially by his preaching an endless succession of parish missions, brought about his early death. As if these life-sapping labors weren't suffering enough, Louis had to bear vicious persecution from the clergy and Jansenist heretics,[10] even to the point of being physically attacked and poisoned by them. Despite all this, our indomitable warrior kept advancing on the battlefield, continuously preaching his trademark path to Jesus through Mary. In fact, when leaders in the Church in France thought they had put an end to his work, Louis walked the thousand-mile journey to Rome and asked the Pope for his wisdom and counsel. The Pope not only told him to go back to France and continue preaching but awarded him the title "Apostolic Missionary." Obediently and joyfully, our saint returned to France where he continued to preach, write, and patiently bear his many sufferings out of love for Jesus, Mary, and souls.

St. Louis's passion and zeal lit a fire in a young Karol Wojtyła, the future Pope John Paul II. A few years before his death, the Pope was able to realize a lifelong dream and visit de Montfort's tomb. He said on that occasion, "I am happy to begin my pilgrimage in France under the sign of this great figure.

You know that I owe much to this saint, and to his *True Devotion to the Blessed Virgin.*"[11]

Now what about us? Do we have a fire in our hearts as we begin this retreat? We should. Or at least we should strive for it. Desire and generosity are key ingredients to making a successful retreat. May Mary intercede for us, and may the Holy Spirit fill us with a passion to conscientiously make these days of retreat, despite any fatigue, distractions, or obstacles. And let's remember that what we may have to endure in terms of the discipline of prayer is nothing compared to what St. Louis went through, and he'll be interceding for us. Relying on his intercession and that of the Mother of God, let's resolve right now to dedicate ourselves to this retreat with the intensity and zeal of a Celtic warrior — though without all the face-paint and screaming.

Today's Prayer:
Come, Holy Spirit, living in Mary.
Help me to make this retreat with generosity and zeal.

DAY 2
St. Louis's Influence on the Church

There's a story from St. Louis de Montfort's life that particularly expresses his passion, which we pondered just yesterday. In the town of Pontchâteau, St. Louis inspired the peasants to build a huge monument to the Passion of Christ on a neighboring hill. For 15 months, hundreds of peasants volunteered their skills and labor to build it. When completed, it stood as a massive structure, a real labor of love, and on the day before it was supposed to be dedicated by the bishop, word got back to Louis that his enemies had convinced the government to destroy it. (They had lied to the authorities, saying that the structure was actually meant to be a fortress against the government.) When Louis received this disappointing news, he told the thousands of people who had gathered for the blessing ceremony, "We had hoped to build a Calvary here. Let us build it in our hearts. Blessed be God."

One thing about doing the Lord's work: It doesn't always turn out according to our plans. For example, St. Louis surely had planned that his monument to Christ would last more than a day. Yet the saint obediently accepted the destruction of his plans and blessed God. Because of this kind of detachment from his own will and attachment to God's, Louis became an instrument used by God to accomplish even mightier works. So, although his physical monument was destroyed, Louis's teaching eventually became a huge edifice in the Church that exercised great influence on many Popes and on Catholic spirituality. Indeed, de Montfort's passionate labors paid off in the end, even if he didn't see the fruit himself.

As we are just beginning our preparation for consecration to Jesus through Mary, let's ponder some of the support various Popes have given to St. Louis's teaching. May the testimony of their support strengthen our resolve to journey on to Consecration Day, and may it help us to trust that our consecration truly will bear great fruit in our lives, even if we don't yet fully understand how.

- **Blessed Pope Pius IX** (1846-1878) stated that St. Louis's devotion to Mary is the best and most acceptable form.

- **Pope Leo XIII** (1878-1903) not only beatified de Montfort in 1888 but granted a Church indulgence to Catholics who consecrate themselves to Mary using de Montfort's formula. Moreover, this Pope was reportedly so influenced by St. Louis's efforts to spread the Rosary that he wrote 11 encyclicals on this preeminent Marian devotion.

- **Pope St. Pius X** (1903-1914), like Leo XIII, also recommended de Montfort's teaching on Mary to the faithful. In fact, he granted a plenary indulgence *in perpetuum* (in perpetuity) to anyone who would pray de Montfort's formula for Marian consecration, and he offered his own apostolic blessing to anyone who would simply read *True Devotion*. This Pope so strongly encouraged the faithful to follow de Montfort's path of Marian devotion because he himself had experienced its power. In fact, in his Marian encyclical *Ad Diem Illum*, the saintly Pope expressed his own dependence on de Montfort in writing it, which becomes obvious when one compares it with *True Devotion*. The Pope's encyclical continually reflects the tone and spirit of de Montfort's classic work as evidenced by sentences like this: "There is no surer or easier way than Mary in uniting all men with Christ."

- **Pope Pius XI** (1922-1939) simply stated, "I have practiced this devotion ever since my youth."

- **Venerable Pope Pius XII** (1939-1958) canonized St. Louis in 1947 and, in his homily for the Mass of canonization, referred to de Montfort's Marian teaching as "solid and right." Then, when the Pope addressed the pilgrims who had come for the canonization, he said that de Montfort leads us to Mary and from Mary, to Jesus, thus summarizing the meaning of Marian consecration.

- **Blessed Pope John Paul II** (1978-2005) promoted de Montfort's teaching more than any other Pope. We'll learn more about this during the fourth week of the retreat. It's enough here to recall two amazing facts: First, that John Paul's papal motto was *Totus Tuus* ("totally yours"), which he took directly from de Montfort's shorter prayer of consecration; second, that John Paul described his reading of *True Devotion to Mary* as a "decisive turning point" in his life.

Today's Prayer:
> *Come, Holy Spirit, living in Mary.*
>> *Prepare me to give myself fully to living out this true and solid devotion.*

DAY 3
De Montfort's Consecration (Part One)

Okay, so on the first day of this week, we asked for a greater passion and zeal in making our preparation for consecration. Then, yesterday, we pondered the incredible influence that de Montfort's brief life has had on the Church. The powerful testimony of authorities no less than Popes should have further fired our zeal and gotten us reflecting, "What is this amazingly influential teaching of a priest who only lived to be 43?" Of course, it's his teaching on Marian consecration, but what exactly does this mean?

Recall the summary of Marian consecration in the introduction to this retreat. There I presented consecration as our giving a "yes" to Mary, allowing her to fulfill in us her God-given task of forming us into other Christs. And that's all true. But there's more. Saint Louis gives two key emphases in his teaching on Marian consecration that expand what we've already read about it. These two emphases are (1) a renewal of our baptismal vows and (2) a particularly intimate gift of ourselves to Mary. Let's look at each of these in turn (one today and one tomorrow).

The day of our Baptism is the most significant in each of our lives. It's when we poor, sinful creatures are not only cleansed of sin but also given the amazing dignity and honor of being transformed into sons and daughters of the almighty God. On that joyous occasion, before we received this amazing grace, we solemnly promised (or if we were infants, others promised in our name) to reject Satan, and then we (or others in our name) professed our faith and commitment to Jesus Christ. Then, every Easter, we solemnly renew this promise and commitment. But do we keep it? Are we true to our word? No. We all sin. Sadly, we all give in to Satan's "pomps and works" and reject Christ, at least in little ways.

Why does this happen? The simple answer is original sin: We have a fallen nature and we're prone to sin. That's true, but St. Louis invites us to go deeper and examine our consciences. If we do, we'll discover that a principal reason why we fall into sin is because of forgetfulness, forgetfulness of our promise and commitment to Christ at Baptism. De Montfort suggests that if we were to personally and sincerely renew our baptismal vows and place them in the hands of Mary, then this act alone would go a long way in helping us overcome sin in our lives. Therefore, he makes such a renewal of vows an essential element of his prayer of consecration. In fact, in the very first paragraph of this prayer, he has us address Mary and pray to her as follows:

> I, (name), a faithless sinner, renew and ratify today in thy hands the vows of my Baptism; I renounce forever Satan, his pomps and works; and I give myself entirely to Jesus Christ, the Incarnate Wisdom, to carry my cross after Him all the days of my life, and to be more faithful to Him than I have ever been before.[12]

So, St. Louis has us attack sin right at its root — Satan and his pomps and works — has us recommit our lives to Christ, and has us do all of this with and through Mary. Why through Mary? Because God has put enmity between her and Satan (see Gen 3:15), and Satan can't stand her. In fact, according to St. Louis, Satan fears her not only more than the angels and saints but, in a sense, even more than God himself! Why? Because, as he puts it, "Satan, being proud, suffers infinitely more from being beaten and punished by a little and humble handmaid of God, and her humility humbles him more than the divine power."[13] So, de Montfort gives us a practical and effective way to overcome sin in our lives: formally renounce Satan and recommit ourselves to Christ, through Mary.

We'll hear more about Mary's power over evil on the last day of this week. Tomorrow, we'll reflect on the second element of St. Louis's consecration, the particularly intimate gift of ourselves to Mary. Today, let's reflect on the promise we made at our Baptism to reject Satan and to love and follow Christ.

Today's Prayer:
> *Come, Holy Spirit, living in Mary.*
>> *Give me the grace to reject Satan and follow Christ more closely.*

DAY 4

De Montfort's Consecration (Part Two)

Yesterday, I said that St. Louis gives two special emphases in his teaching on Marian consecration: (1) a renewal of our baptismal vows and (2) a particularly intimate gift of ourselves to Mary. We covered the first emphasis yesterday. Now let's look at the second, beginning by asking the question, "Why should we give ourselves to Mary?"

We should give ourselves to Mary in imitation of our Lord and Savior, Jesus Christ. After all, didn't Jesus give himself to Mary from the moment of the Incarnation? Yes, he did. And aren't we called to imitate Christ? Yes, we are. But isn't Mary a creature? Yes she is, but she's unique. Not only is Mary free from sin and totally conformed to God's will, but by God's will and good pleasure — as we learned from the introduction — Mary has a special role in our sanctification. Therefore, we should give ourselves to the Mother of God, so she can help form us into saints, into other Christs. We should give her our yes. But St. Louis takes all of this a step further. His yes to Mary is particularly deep, a profoundly intimate gift of himself to Mary:

> This devotion consists, then, in giving ourselves entirely to Our Lady, in order to belong entirely to Jesus through her. We must give her (1) our body, with all its senses and its members; (2) our soul, with all its powers; (3) our exterior goods of fortune, whether present or to come; (4) our interior and spiritual goods, which are our merits and our virtues, and our good works, past, present, and future.[14]

This fourth point is most interesting. By this aspect of our consecration to Mary — according to St. Louis — our gift of self to her goes even beyond what is required when people offer themselves to God through religious vows. For instance, by virtue of the vows of poverty, chastity, and obedience, a religious sister does not give God the right to dispose of the grace of all her good works nor does she give up her merits. Allow me to bring into better focus just how radical a gift of oneself this Marian consecration really is.

First, in regard to others, if we give Mary the right to dispose of the graces of our good works, then this means we cannot unconditionally apply such graces to whomever we choose. So, for instance, if I make such an offering to Mary, I cannot insist that the graces from a sickness I am offering up go to the person I want them applied to. Second, in regard to ourselves, if we consecrate ourselves to Mary, then when we die, we won't get to appear before God clothed with the merits of our prayers and good works. In fact, we'll have to appear before God with empty hands, because we will have given all our merits to Mary.

If the radical nature of this offering has got you worried, don't be worried. Tomorrow, we'll see why this offering is not to be feared, and in fact, why it's incredibly beautiful and completely worth it. Until then, we can reflect on the second part of de Montfort's formula for Marian consecration, which speaks of this intimate gift of ourselves to Mary:

> In the presence of all the heavenly court, I choose you this day for my Mother and Queen. I deliver and consecrate to you, as your slave, my body and soul, my goods, both interior and exterior, and even the value of all my good actions, past, present, and future; leaving to you the entire and full right of disposing of me, and all that belongs to me, without exception, according to your good pleasure, for the greater glory of God, in time and eternity.[15]

Today's Prayer:
   Come, Holy Spirit, living in Mary.
   Help me to give myself entirely to Jesus through Mary.

Should We Really Give Mary *Everything*?
(Part One)

The second part of de Montfort's formula of consecration says that we should give Mary *everything*, including "our interior and spiritual goods, which are our merits and our virtues, and our good works, past, present, and future." Isn't this a bit too much? No. It's perfect. It's beautiful. Let's see why by learning how the offering affects others and ourselves.

In regard to others, when we fully consecrate ourselves to Mary, we lose the unconditional right to distribute the value of our prayers and good actions to others. In other words, we give the rights to the grace (merit) of our prayers to Mary. We're telling her, "Mary, I give you the right to distribute the grace of my prayers as you see fit."

Making such a gift to Mary has a big benefit. It ensures that the grace of our prayers will be used in the best way possible. It works like this: Because of her unique vantage point from heaven, and on account of her most intimate communion with her Divine Son, Mary can best determine which people are most in need of our prayers. For instance, seeing some forgotten person in China about to die in despair, Mary can take the grace of our prayers (and "offered up" sufferings) and use it to help that dying person to trust in God and accept his mercy.

Now, perhaps this idea has got some of us thinking:

Well, that's great. I'm happy to help the dying person in China, whom I don't know, but I'd be disappointed if I therefore couldn't use the grace of my prayers and good works to help the people I do know, like my family and friends. I'm worried that if I give Mary the right to distribute the grace of my prayers and good works, then I thereby lose the right to pray for those whom I especially love, even if they're less in need than other people in the world.

This is a legitimate concern, but there's no need to worry. Why? For two reasons: First, Mary makes the good things we give her more perfect. In other words, she augments, increases, and purifies the spiritual gifts and merits we give her. When we give them to her, because she makes them more perfect, there's more grace and merit to go around. St. Louis uses an unforgettable analogy to explain this:

> It is as if a peasant, wishing to gain the friendship and benevolence of the king, went to the queen and presented her with a fruit which was his whole revenue, in order that she might present it to the king. The queen, having accepted the poor little offering from the peasant, would place the fruit on a large and beautiful dish of gold, and so, on the peasant's behalf, would present it to the king. Then the fruit, however unworthy in itself to be a king's present, would become worthy of his majesty because of the dish of gold on which it rested and the person who presented it.[16]

Here's the second reason we shouldn't worry: Mary is never outdone in generosity. So, if we're so generous as to give her the right to distribute the grace of our prayers and good works, she'll surely be especially generous to our loved ones. In fact, she'll take even better care of our loved ones than we ourselves can. For instance, let's say one of our family members or friends is in need of prayer, and we don't know it. Well, Mary knows it, and she'll make sure that that person doesn't go without. Giving Mary the right to distribute the grace of our prayers and good works doesn't mean we can't still pray for our loved ones. We can and should pray for them. It's just that we give Mary the final say in deciding to whom and for what purpose the grace of our prayers and good works should be applied.

Remember, Mary is not outdone in generosity. She especially hears the prayers of those of us who have given her everything — including the value of all our good works — and she wants us to tell her of the people and intentions we hold in our hearts. If we've given her everything, is there any doubt that she'll be generous in giving whatever good we ask for to those who are dear to us?[17]

Today's Prayer:
> *Come, Holy Spirit, living in Mary.*
> *Help me be generous in giving all I have to Mary.*

DAY 6
Should We Really Give Mary *Everything?*
(Part Two)

Okay, so yesterday we looked at how, when we fully consecrate ourselves to Mary, we give up the right to distribute the grace of our prayers and merits to others. But we saw that it all works out even better in the end. Now, today, we turn to ourselves. Isn't it crazy to give to Mary all the value of our good actions and prayers and so appear before God with empty hands? No, it's not crazy. Remember, Mary is not outdone in generosity. If we give her all our merits, she'll give us all of hers. And that's a big deal.

I once read a story about a saint on earth who had a vision of heaven. In her vision, she saw the saints in heaven and their different degrees of glory. With some saints, she was astonished because they had risen so high in glory as to be worshiping God with the Seraphim, the highest choir of angels. Another time, I read a passage in the *Diary of St. Faustina* in which Faustina had a similar vision of heaven. She related that if we were to see the differences among the degrees of glory in heaven, we would willingly suffer anything on earth just to move one degree higher.[18] After reading these testimonies, I say to myself, "I not only want to go to heaven, but I want to reach the highest degree of glory in heaven that I possibly can." There's an easy way for us to do this: We give Mary everything. We rely not on our own merits but on hers. Saint Louis explains:

> The most holy Virgin ... who never lets herself be outdone in love and liberality, seeing that we give our-

selves entirely to her ... meets us in the same spirit. She also gives her whole self, and gives it in an unspeakable manner, to him who gives all to her. She causes him to be engulfed in the abyss of her graces. She adorns him with her merits; she supports him with her power; she illuminates him with her light; she inflames him with her love; she communicates to him her virtues: her humility, her faith, her purity, and the rest. ... In a word, as that consecrated person is all Mary's, so Mary is all his.[19]

Now, despite these consoling words, one might still be troubled and say, "That's great! I'm all for having a high degree of glory in heaven. But what I'm worried about is purgatory. I'm afraid that if I give away all my merits, even to Mary, then I'll have to suffer in purgatory for a very long time." Saint Louis responds:

This objection, which comes from self-love and ignorance of the generosity of God and His holy Mother, refutes itself. A fervent and generous soul who gives God all he has, without reserve, so that he can do nothing more; who lives only for the glory and reign of Jesus Christ, through His holy Mother, and who makes an entire sacrifice of himself to bring it about — will this generous and liberal soul, I say, be more punished in the other world because it has been more liberal and more disinterested than others? Far, indeed, will that be from the truth! Rather, it is toward that soul ... that Our Lord and His holy Mother are the most liberal in this world and in the other, in the orders of nature, grace, and glory.[20]

Okay, this settles it — and we get a gentle rebuke on top of it all. Saint Louis repeats the important point: Mary is not outdone in generosity! If we are especially generous with her, then she'll be especially generous with us. And he makes another good point: the gentle rebuke. He says that these kinds of concerns come from self-love. So, yes, we should aim high. Yes, we should have holy ambition and want to reach the highest heights of holiness. But our motive should not be self-love; rather, it should be that we want to please God and give great glory to him. We should keep this important point in mind when, tomorrow, we read about some of the awesome benefits of being consecrated to Mary.

Today's Prayer:
> *Come, Holy Spirit, living in Mary.*
> *Help me to give great glory to God by giving all I have to Mary.*

DAY 7
A Quick, Easy, and Secure Way to Holiness

For the last two days, we've learned about some beautiful benefits of being consecrated to Jesus through Mary, benefits both to ourselves and to those who are closest to us. Today, on this final day of meditation on the teaching of St. Louis, we're going to focus on other benefits of Marian consecration. Specifically, we're going to learn about how Marian consecration is a quick, easy, and secure way to holiness. As we read about this, we should keep in mind that the gift of these benefits doesn't entitle us to just kick back and take it easy. (This would be the self-love that St. Louis rebuked during yesterday's reading.) Rather, when we see God's generosity in giving us such a great gift as Marian consecration, we should strive all the more ardently to live it out and grow in holiness.

Let's start with the quick and easy part: The way of consecration to Jesus through Mary is a quick and easy way to holiness. And what is holiness? Dying to self. And this definitely is not easy. Still, Marian consecration is a relatively quick and easy way along a path that by its very nature isn't easy and often takes a long time. Saint Louis introduces this way as follows:

> As there are secrets of nature by which natural operations are performed more easily, in a short time

and at little cost, so also are there secrets in the order of grace by which supernatural operations, such as ridding ourselves of self, filling ourselves with God, and becoming perfect, are performed more easily.[21]

So how do we follow this quick and easy way? By giving ourselves to Jesus through Mary. Mary leads us to Jesus and makes the road to holiness quick and easy, even though she doesn't take away our crosses. In fact, those who are particularly beloved by Mary often have more crosses than others, but Mary makes the crosses sweet and light:

> [I]t is quite true that the most faithful servants of the Blessed Virgin, being also her greatest favorites, receive from her the greatest graces and favors of Heaven, which are crosses. But I maintain that it is also the servants of Mary who carry these crosses with more ease, more merit, and more glory. That which would stay the progress of another a thousand times over, or perhaps would make him fall, does not once stop their steps, but rather enables them to advance; because that good Mother, all full of grace and of the unction of the Holy Spirit, prepares her servants' crosses with so much maternal sweetness and pure love as to make them gladly acceptable, no matter how bitter they may be in themselves; ... [it's] just as a person would not be able to eat unripe fruits without a great effort which he could hardly keep up, unless they had been preserved in sugar.[22]

We make more progress in a brief period of submission to and dependence on Mary than in whole years of following our own will and relying upon ourselves.[23]

By this practice, faithfully observed, you will give Jesus more glory in a month than by any other practice, however difficult, in many years.[24]

[True devotees of Mary] have such facility in carrying
the yoke of Jesus Christ that they feel almost nothing
of its weight.[25]

So, the way of Marian consecration truly is quick and easy,
relatively speaking. As St. Louis says elsewhere, it's like the
difference between a sculptor who makes a statue through long
weeks of hard labor, hammering away with a chisel and another
artist who makes the same statue quickly and easily by using a
mold. Mary is the mold that forms us most perfectly, quickly,
and easily into other images of Christ.[26]

We'll now close these reflections on the wonderful benefits
of Marian consecration by letting St. Louis describe how this
way is also a *secure* path, meaning that, as we walk it, we're
particularly protected from and defended against evil:

[Mary] puts herself around [her true children], and
accompanies them "like an army in battle array"
(Cant 6:3). Shall a man who has an army of a hundred
thousand soldiers around him fear his enemies? A
faithful servant of Mary, surrounded by her protection
... has still less to fear. This good Mother ... would
rather dispatch battalions of millions of angels to assist
one of her servants than that it should ever be said
that a faithful servant of Mary, who trusted in her, had
had to succumb to the malice, the number, and the
vehemence of his enemies.[27]

Today's Prayer:
Come, Holy Spirit, living in Mary.
    Help me to praise you for such a quick, easy, and secure
    path to holiness!

Week Two
St. Maximilian Kolbe

This week, we'll focus on the example and words of the 20th century apostle of Marian consecration, St. Maximilian Kolbe. Kolbe knew well de Montfort's Marian teaching and spoke enthusiastically about it. In formulating his own expression of true devotion to Mary, he not only deepened several of de Montfort's insights but added many new ideas from his own contemplation of the mystery of Mary. Before we turn to his Marian teaching, let's first get to know the man.

Who are you, St. Maximilian Kolbe?

"Who are you, St. Maximilian Kolbe?"

If we were to ask the saint this question in an interview, we might be disappointed, at least initially. With gentleness and humility, he would probably reply: "Now that question is not so important. What's really important is this one: 'Who are you, *O Immaculate Conception?*'" This answer shouldn't disappoint us if our goal in the interview were to get to know St. Maximilian, for his answer actually tells us a lot about him. In fact, one great passion of his life was to come to know the mystery of Mary, particularly as she revealed herself to St. Bernadette of Lourdes, "I am the Immaculate Conception." Why did she call herself "The Immaculate Conception?" Isn't her name Mary? Tomorrow, we'll begin to reflect on this intriguing mystery. Today, let's see what, in our hypothetical interview, Kolbe wouldn't have answered.

Who is St. Maximilian Kolbe? He's known by many titles: Martyr of Charity, The Saint of Auschwitz, Founder of the Militia Immaculata, Apostle of Mary, and Patron Saint of the 20th Century. But before all this, he was just Raymond, Raymond Kolbe, who in 1894 was born into a poor, Polish farming family. And from the beginning, one wouldn't have guessed he'd eventually be a great saint. In fact, one day, his mother was so frustrated with his behavior that she yelled at him in exasperation: "Raymond, what will become of you?!" This shook the boy to the core. Filled with grief, he immediately turned to the Mother of God, asking her, "What *will* become of me?" Then he went to a church and repeated his question. The future saint recounted what happened next:

> Then the Virgin Mother appeared to me holding in her hands two crowns, one white and one red. She looked at me with love and she asked me if I would like to have them. The white meant that I would remain pure and red that I would be a martyr.
>
> I answered yes, I wanted them. Then the Virgin looked at me tenderly and disappeared.[28]

The white crown of purity came first. Raymond confirmed himself in it when, as Brother Maximilian, he professed religious vows, one of which was chastity. But his purity was not just of the body. For there's another kind of purity: purity of intention. A person practices purity of intention when he directs his thoughts, words, and actions not to himself or another creature but to a divine purpose or mission, and ultimately to God.

Perhaps because of his natural intensity and passion, Kolbe felt a particularly strong desire to give himself to a specific mission or goal. One of his classmates in the minor seminary relates, "He often said that he desired to consecrate his entire life to a great idea."[29] Kolbe's "great idea" eventually crystallized into what he called the "Militia Immaculata," which he started in 1917 with six of his fellow seminarians. The "M.I.," as they called it, truly was a "great idea," at least in the sense of its ambition. Its goal was nothing less than to bring the whole world to God through Christ under the generalship of Mary Immaculate, and to do so as quickly as possible. Fulfilling this mission through obedience to God's will, in union with Mary Immaculate, was Kolbe's entire concern — his pure intention — and he sacrificed everything for its accomplishment, which brings us to the red crown.

In 1941, after decades of incredibly fruitful apostolic labors in Poland and Japan, Kolbe was arrested by the Gestapo and sent to the Auschwitz concentration camp. Before his arrest, his brother Franciscans had pleaded with him to go into hiding. He said he was grateful for their loving hearts but couldn't follow their advice. Later, he explained why, "I have a mission — the Immaculata has a mission to fulfill."[30] That mission was accomplished on the eve of the feast of Mary's Assumption into heaven, when, after having volunteered to take the place of a prisoner condemned to starvation, the impatient Nazis finished Kolbe off with a lethal injection. Thus, St. Maximilian died a martyr of charity and received his second crown from his Immaculata.

Today's Prayer:
> *Come, Holy Spirit, living in Mary.*
> *Make me pure in body and spirit and help me to die*
> *to myself.*

DAY 9
Who are you, O Immaculate Conception?
(Part One)

Yesterday, when I mentioned St. Maximilian's arrest by the Gestapo, I left out a remarkable detail that will be important for today's reflection: Two hours before his arrest, the future saint penned the single most important theological reflection of his life. It was nothing less than *the answer* that had eluded him for so many years, the answer to the question he had pondered over and over from the earliest days of his religious life: " *Who are you, O Immaculate Conception?*" In today's reflection, we'll begin to unpack this remarkable document, but before we do, let's pause and say a silent prayer to the Immaculata, asking for the grace to receive Kolbe's wisdom.

The document begins as follows:

> IMMACULATE CONCEPTION. These words fell from the lips of the Immaculata herself. Hence, they must tell us in the most precise and essential manner who she really is. ...
> Who then are you, O Immaculate Conception?[31]

Good question, but still no answer. Later in the document, Kolbe points out a simple but key point: At the apparitions in Lourdes, Mary didn't say to St. Bernadette "I was immaculately conceived" but rather "*I am the Immaculate Conception.*" This seems to be a problem. After all, Mary *was* immaculately conceived. In other words, through a special grace from God, she was conceived in the womb of her mother, St. Anne, without any stain of original sin by the foreseen merits of her Son.[32] So why does she speak so strangely? Why does she make the grace she received at her conception *her very name*? Doesn't this almost seem as if she were making herself divine? Clearly, Mary is not God. Kolbe wrestled with this apparent "divinity problem" for decades, and it led to the following solution.

The Immaculate Conception is divine. But the one I'm talking about isn't Mary. It's the Holy Spirit. In other words, Kolbe believed there are two "Immaculate Conceptions": Mary and the Holy Spirit. Mary is the *created* Immaculate Conception and the Holy Spirit is the *uncreated* Immaculate Conception. In other words, before there was the *created* Immaculate Conception (Mary), for all eternity there is the *uncreated* Immaculate Conception, the One who for all eternity "springs" from God the Father and God the Son as an uncreated conception of Love and who is the "prototype of all the conceptions that multiply life throughout the whole universe."[33] So, "the Father begets; the Son is begotten; the Spirit is the 'conception' that springs from their love."[34]

Now, the Holy Spirit is a "conception" in the sense of being the Life and Love that springs from the love of the Father and the Son — in some analogous way, there's the conception of children who "spring" from the love of husband and wife. The Holy Spirit is an "immaculate" conception because, being God, he is obviously without sin. And finally, the Holy Spirit is an "eternal, uncreated" conception because, again, he is God.

Okay, so this covers Kolbe's teaching that the Holy Spirit is the Immaculate Conception, but why does Mary call herself by the same name? We'll leave this question for tomorrow.

Today's Prayer:
Come, Holy Spirit, living in Mary.
Unveil for me the meaning of the Immaculate
Conception.

DAY 10
Who are you, O Immaculate Conception?
(Part Two)

So the Holy Spirit is the *uncreated* Immaculate Conception and Mary is the *created* Immaculate Conception. Why not make it easier and just say that the Holy Spirit is the Immaculate Conception and Mary was immaculately conceived? Again, it's all because of Lourdes. Blame St. Bernadette!

In all seriousness, we should thank both St. Bernadette and St. Kolbe profusely, because their fidelity to grace is now opening up for us a glorious truth that undergirds the whole theology of Marian consecration. This truth has to do with *the union between the Holy Spirit and Mary.* Kolbe explains this in a passage that is long and difficult but incredibly rich and deserving of deep reflection:

> What type of union is this [between the Holy Spirit and Mary]? It is above all an interior union, a union of her essence with the "essence" of the Holy Spirit. The Holy Spirit dwells in her, lives in her. This was true from the first instant of her existence. It was always true; it will always be true.
>
> In what does this life of the Spirit in Mary consist? He himself is uncreated Love in her; the Love of the Father and of the Son, the Love by which God loves himself, the very love of the Most Holy Trinity. He is a fruitful Love, a "Conception." Among creatures made in God's image the union brought about by married love is the most intimate of all (see Mt 19:6). In a much more precise, more interior, more essential manner, the Holy Spirit lives

in the soul of the Immaculata, in the depths of her very
being. He makes her fruitful, from the very first instant
of her existence, all during her life, and for all eternity.

This eternal "Immaculate Conception" (which
is the Holy Spirit) produces in an immaculate manner
divine life itself in the womb (or depths) of Mary's
soul, making her the Immaculate Conception, the
human Immaculate Conception. And the virginal
womb of Mary's body is kept sacred for him; there he
conceives in time — because everything that is material
occurs in time — the human life of the Man-God.

... If among human beings the wife takes the
name of her husband because she belongs to him, is
one with him, becomes equal to him and is, with him,
the source of new life, with how much greater reason
should the name of the Holy Spirit, who is the divine
Immaculate Conception, be used as the name of her
in whom he lives as uncreated Love, the principle of
life in the whole supernatural order of grace?[35]

In light of this remarkable passage, I'd like to make three
points. First, ponder it again, deeply and prayerfully. As you
do, keep in mind that these are the parting words of one of the
greatest Marian saints of all time, answering the very question
to which he dedicated his life and energies. Second, if it seems
that Kolbe has gone a bit overboard with this talk of Mary and
her union with the Holy Spirit, don't worry. Pope Paul VI went
out of his way to reassure the faithful that Kolbe's teaching is
sound.[36] Third, if you only get one point from this challenging
passage, may it be this: Mary is the Spouse of the Holy Spirit.
In fact, her union with the Holy Spirit is even deeper than what
we understand by a spousal relationship. We'll pick up this
thread tomorrow.

Today's Prayer:
> *Come, Holy Spirit, living in Mary.*
> > *Unveil for me the meaning of the Immaculate*
> > *Conception.*

DAY 11
The Immaculata Always Does God's Will, Perfectly

Yesterday, we learned about the intimate union between the Holy Spirit and Mary, the uncreated and created Immaculate Conceptions. Now we may be thinking, "That's nice, but what follows from it?" Here's what follows: Mary does the will of God perfectly — and this is a big deal. Let's take a step back and put this into context by looking at the *big* picture of reality.

According to St. Thomas Aquinas, all of creation makes one big, circular movement from God and back to God, referred to by theologians as "The Great Circle of Being." Aquinas writes:

> Issuing from the Primary Principle, creatures accomplish a sort of circuit, a gyratory movement, such that all things when they tend to their proper end are returning to the Principle whence they came forth. ... We were created by the Son and by the Holy Spirit; and hence it is by them that we are brought back to our end.[37]

Now, St. Maximilian Kolbe, being the good theologian that he was, describes this big picture structure of reality in a similar way. He begins by pointing to our own experience of the world:

> Everywhere in this world we notice action ... departure and return; going away and coming back; separation and reunion. The separation always looks forward to union, which is creative. All this is simply an image of the Blessed Trinity in the activity of creatures.[38]

What Kolbe describes here really is true. It's the structure of the cosmos. Everything has come forth from God and is going back to God, more or less perfectly. This movement is sometimes called the great "Exit and Return." Although Kolbe uses the term "separation" instead of "exit," he's got the same idea:

First, God creates the universe; that is something like a separation. Creatures, by following the natural law implanted in them by God, reach their perfection, become like him, and go back to him. Intelligent creatures [human beings] love him in a conscious manner; through this love they unite themselves more and more closely with him, and so find their way back to him.[39]

Among all creatures in the universe, Kolbe believes that the Immaculata deserves special mention:

The creature most completely filled with this love, filled with God himself, was the Immaculata, who never contracted the slightest stain of sin, who never departed in the least from God's will. United to the Holy Spirit as his spouse, she is one with God in an incomparably more perfect way than can be predicated of any other creature.[40]

Let's reflect for a moment on this vision of reality: First, everything going forth from God. Think of all creation. God speaks, and it goes forth from him. Then, plants and animals return to God by fulfilling their natures, by being what they were created to be. They do this without thinking or deliberating and with a sort of ease. It happens by a kind of instinctual autopilot. Human beings, on the other hand, are different. While there are times when we act by instinct, we also act in a way different from the animals. We act by reason and will, and we're conscious as we do so, present to ourselves as we act. This is what it means to be made in the image of God: We can know God and love him. And whereas the animals do God's will by instinct, we can do his will freely and consciously.

The problem is, we abuse the freedom God gave us. We don't always choose his will, and so we don't return to him as we should. We sin. And if we sin gravely and don't fully repent, then we don't make it back to God. This is a great tragedy of human life. But thanks be to God! For he sent his only Son and the power of his Spirit to save us, to bring us back home to our Father in heaven. And thank God that after the fall of the human race, he made a creature who was conceived without sin and who is freely and perfectly conformed to his will, for she is perfectly united with the Holy Spirit. She helps us poor sinners along the way. She helps us to overcome the tragedy of sin. She leads us to do God's will, return to God, and become saints. We'll hear more about this tomorrow.

Today's Prayer:
> *Come, Holy Spirit, living in Mary.*
> *Renew the face of the earth, so that all creation may*
> *return to God.*

DAY 12
Who Are You, O Holy Saints of God?

Saint Maximilian used to give spiritual conferences to the new men in his religious community, the novices. One day, he taught them a lesson they would never forget: "How to become a Saint." The future saint began by telling his listeners that sanctity isn't so hard. It's the result of a simple equation, which he wrote on the blackboard: "$W + w = S$." The capital W stands for God's Will. The small w stands for our wills. When the two wills are united, they equal Sanctity.

This lesson wasn't just for the novices. Kolbe repeated it over and over, in different ways, to his whole community. In Poland, Kolbe had founded the world's largest Franciscan monastery, which he named *Niepokolanow* ("City of the Immaculate"), and he continually urged the more than 600 friars there to become soldier saints for God under the generalship of Mary Immaculate. Why under Mary Immaculate? Because, among creatures, she alone does the will of God perfectly. Therefore, when our wills are united with hers, they're necessarily united to God's will. Here are just two of the countless examples of how Kolbe would make this most important point:

Let us pray much that we would understand more and more what the Immaculata said at the Annunciation: "Behold, the handmaid of the Lord, let it be done unto me [*fiat mihi*] according to your word." As God wills, so be it. In this thought, all happiness is contained, already here on earth, all destiny fulfilled. ...

Let us beg our Blessed Mother that she might teach us how our soul might be a "handservant" of the Lord, as was her own. God did not reveal Himself directly to the Mother of God, but rather through a messenger. We too have divine messengers. ... Let us pray that we would know how to say to every one of these messengers: God's will be done. And in this is everything that we are placed upon this earth to learn.[41]

To be one in will with Mary of the great *fiat*, the only human being whose will has never deviated by her choice from God's, is to be perfectly united to the will of God. And it is this alignment of your will with his that is the pressing business of your life.[42]

Doing God's will is not easy — unless we have the Immaculata's help, "Through the Immaculata we can become great saints, and what is more, in an easy way."[43] Becoming a saint was Kolbe's number one goal. Literally. In his retreat notes before his ordination to the priesthood, he made a list of his spiritual goals. The first goal reads, "I wish to be a saint and a great saint."[44] He knew the Immaculata would help him and even make the path to great sanctity an easy one.

How does Mary make sanctity easy? We read many reasons for this last week, during our closing reflection on St. Louis de Montfort's teaching. But Kolbe emphasized another reason why Mary makes sanctity easy. It has to do with her being the Mediatrix of all grace, an idea he expresses in his formula for Marian consecration, "God has willed to entrust the entire order of mercy to [Mary]."[45] It's God's will that she distribute his graces. Why? Because it's God's will to unite himself to Mary by his Holy Spirit, "The Holy Spirit does not act except through the Immaculata, his spouse. Hence, she is the Mediatrix of all the graces of the Holy Spirit."[46] And hence, it's "easy" to become holy when we stay close to and ask for graces from the one whose very job it is to distribute them for God.

We can get a better idea of Mary as Mediatrix of grace if we look at her image on the miraculous medal, which comes to us through her apparitions to St. Catherine Labouré. Kolbe was deeply moved by this image, because it depicts Mary standing on a globe with rays of light (graces) streaming from the rings on her fingers. In one of the apparitions, Catherine noticed that rays did not stream from all of Mary's rings. Mary explained that the rays and graces were available but did not come because nobody asked for them. Kolbe's way is not just to ask for these graces but to allow Mary to take us completely into her hands, so as to make us channels of these very graces for the whole world. We'll learn more about this way tomorrow.

Today's prayer:
> *Come, Holy Spirit, living in Mary.*
> *Unite my will to the will of the Immaculata,*
> *which is one with your will.*

DAY 13
To Be an Instrument — Rather, to be Instruments

Again, St. Maximilian didn't just want to ask for graces from the Immaculata. He wanted to *be* the graces of the Immaculata. He didn't just want to do the will of the Immaculata. He wanted to *be* the will of the Immaculata. Wait, *be* the graces and the will of the Immaculata? Isn't this a bit too much? Not according to Kolbe's reasoning. He figured, "Well, if people can give themselves over to Satan to be possessed by him and be his instruments of evil, why can't people give themselves over to God to be possessed by him and be his instruments of love?" He further reasoned that, more than anyone, the Immaculata is "possessed" by the Holy Spirit,[47] so why not ask to be "possessed" by her so as to be perfectly united to God's will? In other words, it wasn't enough for him just to be Mary's "slave," as St. Louis de Montfort often put it. He wanted something deeper. He wanted to be an *instrument* in the hands of the Immaculata.

To be an instrument in the hands of the Immaculata. This is the central idea to Kolbe's whole vision of Marian consecration. Thus, he writes it directly into his prayer of consecration, "Let me be a fit instrument in your immaculate and merciful hands." To what purpose? The conversion of *the entire world*.

Come on. Kolbe is getting a little carried away, right? I mean, what can one man do? But this gets to his main point, his master strategy. His own piece wasn't the only part of his master plan. In fact, he wanted to raise up *a whole army* of fighting knights and soldiers who give themselves to be instruments in the grace-filled hands of the Immaculata. He wanted to build a "Militia Immaculata," which he describes as follows:

> The Knights of the Immaculata seek to become ever more truly the property of the Immaculata; to belong to her in an ever more perfect way and under every aspect without any exception. They wish to develop their understanding of what it means to belong to her so that they may enlighten, reinvigorate, and set on fire the souls living in their own environment, and make them similar to themselves. They desire to conquer these souls for the Immaculata, so that in their turn they may belong to her without reserve and may in this manner win an ever greater number of souls to her — may win the entire world, in fact, and do so in the shortest possible time.[48]

What genius! Notice the brilliant logic that undergirds Kolbe's whole strategy: If we really love God, if we truly long to work for his kingdom, then we should find the quickest and easiest way to become saints, and thereby return to him. Now, the quickest and easiest way to do this — as we learned from de Montfort — is through Marian consecration.

Yet Kolbe takes it further: He didn't just stop with himself. He didn't keep the great saint-making secret to himself. Look at it this way: What's better, one saint or two? A thousand saints or a million? Think of what a million saints fully consecrated to Mary could do. Imagine if Mary had a million instruments through whom she could fulfill the perfect will of God. It's an amazing thought. So, Kolbe exclaims, "Teach others this way! Conquer more souls for the Immaculata!" If this is the quickest, easiest way to become a saint, then it's also the quickest, easiest way to conquer the whole world for Christ, if only we teach others about it. So, Kolbe says, "Let's get to work!" Yes, let's begin by learning to live this consecration ourselves, and then bring others into it.

Okay, so first things first. We need to learn to live this consecration to the Immaculata. We need to "belong to her in an ever more perfect way." How do we do this? Simple. We learn to love the Immaculata. How? *By relying on her powerful intercession, experiencing her tender care, speaking to her from our hearts, letting ourselves be led by her, having recourse to her in all things, and trusting her completely.* Yes, we should especially trust in the Immaculata and be happy in her. We should follow the example of Kolbe, related to us by one of his religious brothers:

> When things ... were going well, he rejoiced with all his heart with everyone and fervently thanked the Immaculata for the graces received through her intercession. When things went badly he was still happy and used to say, "Why should we be sad? Doesn't the Immaculata, our little mother, know everything that's going on?"[49]

Tomorrow, we'll learn more about Kolbe's form of consecration to "our little mother." Today, let's end by reflecting on his words: "My dear, dear brothers, our dear little, little mother, the Immaculate Mary, can do anything for us. We are her children. Turn to her. She will overcome everything."[50]

Today's Prayer:
> *Come, Holy Spirit, living in Mary.*
> *Prepare me to be a fit instrument in the hands of*
> *the Immaculata.*

DAY 14
Kolbe's Prayer of Consecration

To conclude this week's reflections on St. Maximillian's teaching on Marian consecration, it will be good for us to get to know his actual prayer of consecration. We'll now look at it in its three parts: (1) an invocation, (2) a plea to Mary, that she will receive us as her property, (3) a plea to Mary, that she will use us to gain other souls for her.

The prayer begins with an invocation:

O Immaculata, Queen of heaven and earth, refuge of sinners and our most loving Mother, God has willed to entrust the entire order of mercy to you.[51]

Here we have Kolbe's favorite title for Mary, the "Immaculata." As we learn from her apparition at Lourdes, this is her identity. For Kolbe, this is her most important identity, because it highlights her intimate union with the Holy Spirit. This invocation also brings in another part of Mary's identity: Mother. Mary is the most humble, gentle, tender, and loving mother. Finally, another of Kolbe's favorite titles is alluded to here, namely, Mediatrix of All Grace. For to Mary, "God has willed to entrust the entire order of mercy."

The second part of the consecration prayer expresses a plea that Mary will receive us as her property:

I, (Name), a repentant sinner, cast myself at your feet humbly imploring you to take me with all that I am and have, wholly to yourself as your possession and property. Please make of me, of all my powers of soul and body, of my whole life, death and eternity, whatever most pleases you.[52]

Recall that de Montfort, in his formula of consecration, expanded and elaborated on *what he was giving to Mary*: body, soul, goods, merits, etc. Kolbe means the same thing as de Montfort, but he simplifies it by expressing his gift of himself to Mary with a concise statement: "[T]ake me with all that I am and have." On the flip side, where de Montfort describes the *purpose* of his consecration with the simple, summary statement, "for the greater glory of God," it's Kolbe who expands and elaborates. Thus, in the third part of his consecration prayer, Kolbe describes the purpose of his offering not simply as "the greater glory of God" but as the following:

> If it pleases you, use all that I am and have without reserve, wholly to accomplish what was said of you: "She will crush your head," and, "You alone have destroyed all heresies in the whole world." Let me be a fit instrument in your immaculate and merciful hands for introducing and increasing your glory to the maximum in all the many strayed and indifferent souls, and thus help extend as far as possible the blessed kingdom of the most Sacred Heart of Jesus. For wherever you enter you obtain the grace of conversion and growth in holiness, since it is through your hands that all graces come to us from the most Sacred Heart of Jesus.[53]

The boldness of the first sentence may easily be overlooked, but when we fully take it in, its boldness can be startling. Kolbe is asking Mary to use him to completely crush the reign of Satan! Perhaps he pulls back this incredible ambition (a little) when he says that he wants her to use him to help extend "*as far as possible* the blessed kingdom of the most Sacred Heart of Jesus." Still, his boldness is incredible. He wants Mary to use him as her instrument — as much as possible — to crush Satan and extend the kingdom of God, the kingdom of the love of the Heart of Jesus.

It's interesting that Kolbe homes in on the Heart of Jesus, mentioning it two times. This isn't a passing fancy. For instance, it appears again when he gives the motto of his army of Knights of the Immaculate, the Militia Immaculata: "To lead all men and every individual through Mary to the most Sacred Heart of Jesus."[54] We'll learn more about the Heart of Jesus as a most perfect goal for our spiritual lives when we reflect on Blessed Mother Teresa and her teachings next week.

Today's Prayer:
> *Come, Holy Spirit, living in Mary.*
> *Prepare me to give all to the Immaculata for the sake of the kingdom.*

Blessed Mother Teresa

This week, we'll focus on the example and words of a third great teacher of Marian consecration: Blessed Mother Teresa of Calcutta. She's notable for the way she puts Marian consecration into context. In other words, while de Montfort and Kolbe give us the main details of Marian consecration, Mother Teresa helps us to see it more fully within the big picture of a most intimate relationship with Christ. Although we won't immediately begin reflections on her devotion to Mary, we'll get to them soon enough.

DAY 15
Lover of the Heart of Jesus

Who is Blessed Mother Teresa of Calcutta? She's easy to understand. All we really need to know are two words: "*I thirst.*" These words of the Heart of Jesus, spoken from his agony on the Cross, were Mother's whole concern, her everything — and the same could be said of Our Lady. The deepest desire of the hearts of both Mother Teresa and the Mother of God is to satiate the thirst of the Heart of Jesus for love and for souls. In this sense, Mother Teresa's life is a revelation of the Heart of Mary and presents one of the richest expressions of Marian consecration. We'll reflect on the details of this revelation and example during many of the days that follow, but first let's ponder an overview of her life as a whole.

Mother Teresa's home parish in her native Macedonia was fittingly called "Sacred Heart." Fittingly, because as she herself said, "From childhood, the Heart of Jesus has been my first love."[55] This love may have begun when, at the age of five, she received the Eucharistic Heart of Jesus for the first time. On that occasion, she experienced the Lord's own burning thirst for souls. Over the years, this thirst grew and blossomed into a conviction at the age of 12 that God was calling her to be a missionary. When she was 18, she joined the Institute of the Blessed Virgin Mary (The Loreto Sisters) and applied to go to their missions in Bengal, India, where she was sent the next year. After a year of novitiate, Teresa was assigned to the Loreto community in Calcutta and appointed to teach at St. Mary's

Bengali Medium School for girls. The new sister would serve there for more than a decade and a half.

Mother Teresa's years at St. Mary's were happy ones. She was a joyful, generous, hardworking sister. In fact, she was so generous with the Lord that, with the permission of her spiritual director, she made an extraordinary vow: to refuse Jesus nothing. Five years later, Jesus tested this vow in a big way. On September 10, 1946, while on a train to her yearly retreat, the 36-year-old sister experienced what she described as "a call within a call." The details of this call became clearer in the subsequent weeks and months through a flood of mystical experiences that included visions. At the heart of this call was *the burning thirst of Jesus for love and for souls* and a plea to Teresa to found the Missionaries of Charity religious congregation. Regarding the latter, as if to remind her of the vow she had made, Jesus kept repeating to her, "Wilt thou refuse?"[56]

Mother Teresa did not refuse the Lord. After her retreat, she spoke with her spiritual director and, with his permission, contacted the bishop. When the bishop hesitated to approve her plans, she wrote to him: "Don't delay, Your Grace, don't put it off. … [L]et us take away from the Heart of Jesus His continual suffering."[57] In the same letter, she repeated this idea, "Let us bring joy to the Heart of Jesus, and remove from His Heart those terrible sufferings."[58] Eventually, the bishop gave his approval, and Mother founded the Missionaries of Charity, whose general purpose she described as follows: "To satiate the thirst of Jesus Christ on the Cross for Love and Souls."[59]

From the beginning of the new congregation, Mother Teresa began to experience "such terrible darkness" in her soul "as if everything was dead."[60] At times, it seemed unbearable, and she frequently found herself on the brink of despair. In 1961, she received a light in this darkness. After a conversation with a holy priest, she realized that her painful longing was actually a share in the thirst of Jesus: "For the first time in this 11 years — I have come to love the darkness. — For I believe now that it is a part, a very, very small part of Jesus' darkness and pain on earth."[61] Teresa's experience of darkness and painful longing continued to the end of her life. She found the strength to persevere because, as her spiritual director put it, she realized that the darkness was actually a "mysterious link" that united her to the Heart of Jesus.[62]

What about us? Do we yet realize the mysterious link between the darkness we sometimes experience in our own lives and that of the Lord's suffering? Let us ponder Mother Teresa's words on suffering that come from her own experience and so, like her, become better lovers of the Heart of Jesus:

> Suffering has to come because if you look at the cross, he has got his head bending down — he wants to kiss you — and he has both hands open wide — he wants to embrace you. He has his heart opened wide to receive you. Then when you feel miserable inside, look at the cross and you will know what is happening. Suffering, pain, sorrow, humiliation, feelings of loneliness, are nothing but the kiss of Jesus, a sign that you have come so close that he can kiss you. Do you understand, brothers, sisters, or whoever you may be? Suffering, pain, humiliation — this is the kiss of Jesus. At times you come so close to Jesus on the cross that he can kiss you. I once told this to a lady who was suffering very much. She answered, "Tell Jesus not to kiss me — to stop kissing me." That suffering has to come that came in the life of Our Lady, that came in the life of Jesus — it has to come in our life also. Only never put on a long face. Suffering is a gift from God. It is between you and Jesus alone inside.[63]

Today's Prayer:
> *Come, Holy Spirit, living in Mary.*
> > *Help me to find the love of the Heart of Jesus hidden in the darkness.*

DAY 16
'The Gift God Gave September 10th'

In the overview of Mother Teresa's life that we reflected on yesterday, recall that one crucial event changed everything: the September 10th "call within a call," the experience of Jesus' thirst for love and for souls. For many years, Mother Teresa did not speak about this experience to anyone except her spiritual director. Then, four years before her death, on March 25, 1993, after reading a Lenten message of Pope John Paul II on "I Thirst,"[64] she felt moved to reveal her secret in a letter to her Missionaries of Charity. Because this letter seems to reveal the heart of Mother Teresa better than anything else, I'll now cite it at length, and it will constitute our entire reflection for today:

> After reading Holy Father's letter on "I Thirst," I was struck so much — I cannot tell you what I felt. His letter made me realize more than ever how beautiful is our vocation. ... [W]e are reminding [the] world of His thirst, something that was being forgotten. ... Holy Father's letter is a sign ... to go more into what is this great thirst of Jesus for each one. It is also a sign for Mother, that the time has come for me to speak openly of [the] gift God gave Sept. 10th — to explain [as] fully as I can what means for me the thirst of Jesus. ...
>
> Jesus wants me to tell you again ... how much love He has for each one of you — beyond all you can imagine. I worry some of you still have not really met Jesus — one to one — you and Jesus alone. We may spend time in chapel — but have you seen with the eyes of your soul how He looks at you with love? Do you really know the living Jesus — not from books but from being with Him in your heart? Have you heard the loving words He speaks to you? Ask for the grace, He is longing to give it. Until you can hear Jesus in the silence of your own heart, you will not be able to hear Him saying "I thirst" in the hearts of the poor.

Never give up this daily intimate contact with Jesus as the real living person — not just the idea. How can we last even one day without hearing Jesus say "I love you" — impossible. Our soul needs that as much as the body needs to breathe the air. If not, prayer is dead — meditation only thinking. Jesus wants you each to hear Him — speaking in the silence of your heart.

Be careful of all that can block that personal contact with the living Jesus. The Devil may try to use the hurts of life, and sometimes our own mistakes — to make you feel it is impossible that Jesus really loves you, is really cleaving to you. This is a danger for all of us. And so sad, because it is completely opposite of what Jesus is really wanting, waiting to tell you. Not only that He loves you, but even more — He longs for you. He misses you when you don't come close. He thirsts for you. He loves you always, even when you don't feel worthy. When not accepted by others, even by yourself sometimes — He is the one who always accepts you. My children, you don't have to be different for Jesus to love you. Only believe — you are precious to Him. Bring all you are suffering to His feet — only open your heart to be loved by Him as you are. He will do the rest.

You all know in your mind that Jesus loves you — but in this letter Mother wants to touch your heart instead. … That is why I ask you to read this letter before the Blessed Sacrament, the same place it was written, so Jesus Himself can speak to you each one.

… His words on the wall of every MC chapel ["I Thirst"], they are not from the past only, but alive here and now, spoken to you. Do you believe it? If so, you will hear, you will feel His presence. Let it become as intimate for each of you, just as for Mother — this is the greatest joy you could give me. Mother will try to help you understand — but Jesus Himself must be the one to say to you "I Thirst." Hear your own name. Not just once. Every day. If you listen with your heart, you will hear, you will understand.

Why does Jesus say "I Thirst"? What does it mean? Something so hard to explain in words — if you remember anything from Mother's letter, remember this — "I thirst" is something much deeper than Jesus just saying "I love you." Until you know deep inside that Jesus thirsts for you — you can't begin to know who He wants to be for you. Or who He wants you to be for Him.

… [Our Lady] was the first person to hear Jesus' cry "I Thirst" with St. John, and I am sure Mary Magdalen. Because Our Lady was there on Calvary, she knows how real, how deep is His longing for you and for the poor. Do we know? Do we feel as she? Ask her to teach … . Her role is to bring you face to face, as John and Magdalen, with the love in the Heart of Jesus crucified. Before it was Our Lady pleading with Mother, now it is Mother in her name pleading with you —"listen to Jesus' thirst." Let it be for each … a Word of Life.

How do you approach the thirst of Jesus? Only one secret — the closer you come to Jesus, the better you will know His thirst. "Repent and believe," Jesus tells us. What are we to repent? Our indifference, our hardness of heart. What are we to believe? Jesus thirsts even now, in your heart and in the poor — He knows your weakness, He wants only your love, wants only the chance to love you. He is not bound by time. Whenever we come close to Him — we become partners of Our Lady, St. John, Magdalen. Hear Him. Hear your own name. Make my joy and yours complete.[65]

Today's Prayer:
  Come, Holy Spirit, living in Mary.
    Help me listen to Jesus' thirst.

DAY 17
The Visions of 1947

Several months after Mother Teresa first felt her "call within a call," she experienced three visions that further expressed her calling. In the first vision, she saw a huge crowd of all kinds of people that included the very poor and children. The people in the crowd had their hands raised toward her and were calling out, "Come, come, save us — bring us to Jesus."[66]

In the second vision, the same great crowd was there, and this time Mother Teresa could see the immense sorrow and suffering in their faces. She was kneeling near Our Lady, who was facing the crowd. Although she couldn't see Mary's face, she could hear what she said: "*Take care of them — they are mine. — Bring them to Jesus — carry Jesus to them. — Fear not.*"[67]

In the third vision, the same great crowd was there again, but they were covered in darkness. Despite this, Teresa could see them. Within this scene, Jesus hung on the Cross, and Our Lady was a little distance away. Teresa, as a little child, was just in front of Mary. Mary's left hand rested on Teresa's left shoulder and her right hand held Teresa's right arm. Both of them were facing the Cross, and Jesus spoke to Teresa:

> *I have asked you. They have asked you, and she, My Mother, has asked you. Will you refuse to do this for Me — to take care of them, to bring them to Me?*[68]

Notice the role of Our Lady in these visions. She is there, helping Teresa to hear the desire of the Lord's Heart and to see the suffering of the crowd. She is there as a Mother with her "little child," facing Jesus and the crowd together. She gives comfort and support to Teresa, just as she did to St. John at the foot of the Cross. Father Joseph Langford, MC, co-founder of the Missionaries of Charity Fathers, reflects on the meaning of these visions:

> Without Our Lady, we would be ... alone before the crosses of life, oblivious to Jesus in our midst. In times

of trial, we are often like the poor in Mother Teresa's vision, covered in darkness, unaware that Jesus is there in the midst of us. [W]ithout the fidelity [Our Lady] gave to Mother Teresa, the world would not have heard those words [I thirst], or seen them lived out, today.[69]

It turns out that Our Lady was specially present to Mother Teresa not only in these visions but also during the original, September 10th grace. On the 50th anniversary of that blessed day, Mother shared something new: "If Our Lady had not been with me that day, I never would have known what Jesus meant when he said, 'I thirst.'"[70] What was Teresa getting at? What she meant comes to light when we reflect again on the Marian dimension of the March 25th letter on "I Thirst":

> ... [Our Lady] was the first person to hear Jesus' cry "I Thirst" with St. John, and I am sure Mary Magdalen. Because Our Lady was there on Calvary, she knows how real, how deep is His longing for you and for the poor. Do we know? Do we feel as she? Ask her to teach ... . Her role is to bring you face to face, as John and Magdalen, with the love in the Heart of Jesus crucified. Before it was Our Lady pleading with Mother, now it is Mother in her name pleading with you —"listen to Jesus' thirst."

This passage gets to the heart of Mother Teresa's relationship with Mary, and nothing summarizes it better than this golden line: *[Our Lady's] role is to bring you face to face ... with the love in the Heart of Jesus crucified.*

Today's Prayer:
> *Come, Holy Spirit, living in Mary.*
> > *Bring me face to face with the love in the Heart of Jesus crucified.*

DAY 18
The Immaculate Heart of Mary

Mary's role is to bring us face to face with the love in the Heart of Jesus crucified. But what if when we're there with him, "face to face," we don't feel moved? What if we stand before a crucifix, ponder the Lord's Passion, and feel little or nothing? What if our hearts are hard and insensitive because of our sins? This happens. We all sin, and sin hardens hearts. Aridity and desolation also happen, regardless of our sins. Whatever the reason, our hearts can be cold and unfeeling, and this can be a problem. Thankfully, the one who has a sinless, perfect, immaculate heart will help us. She'll give us her compassionate heart. She'll even let us live in her heart! If only we'll give her ours.

During our week with St. Louis de Montfort, we learned that when we consecrate ourselves to Mary, we give our whole selves to her, and Mary then gives her whole self to us. The emphasis that week was on merits: If we give our merits to Mary, she gives her merits to us. This is a marvelous thing. Yet Mother Teresa gives a bit of a different emphasis to all this. Her concern is with the heart. In other words, her version of a total consecration to Mary focuses on a kind of exchange of hearts: We give Mary our hearts, and she gives us her Immaculate Heart. For Mother Teresa, this gift of Mary's heart through consecration essentially means two things that are expressed by two simple prayers: "Lend me your heart" and "Keep me in your most pure heart."

First, "*Lend me your heart.*" By this prayer, Mother Teresa asked Our Lady to give her the love of her heart. In other words, she says, "Mary, help me to love with the perfect love of your Immaculate Heart." Remember, Mother Teresa's passionate desire was to satiate the thirst of Jesus for love, and she wanted to do this in the best way possible. What better way to love Jesus than with the perfect, humble, immaculate Heart of his mother? Here, Mother Teresa found the secret to living out her vocation to the full: "Mary, lend me your Immaculate Heart."

But can Mary really give us her heart? Of course, there's something piously poetic in this idea. Yet there's truth in it.

When Mother Teresa often said to Mary, "Lend me your heart," she meant it. Did she suppose that the physical organ of her heart would be removed from her body and that Mary would come down from heaven and give her hers? Of course not. The physical organ of the heart is itself but a symbol of a deeper, spiritual reality. "The heart" refers to one's inner life and the seat of the indwelling Holy Spirit. The Holy Spirit. Now we come to the heart of the heart of the matter.

Recall our week with St. Maximilian Kolbe and how he emphasized the bond between the Holy Spirit and Mary. He said that Mary is the spouse of the Holy Spirit and that their union goes even deeper than a spousal union. He went on to say things like this: "The Holy Spirit does not act except through the Immaculata, his spouse. Hence, she is the Mediatrix of all the graces of the Holy Spirit."[71] So, if we want to love Jesus completely, ardently, and perfectly — as did Mother Teresa — then we need his Spirit of Love, and Mary Immaculate brings him to us. Let us pray, "Mary, lend us your Heart. Bring us the Spirit. Pray that our hardened hearts would burn with love for Jesus. Help set our hearts on fire with love for him."

The second prayer is "*Keep me in your most pure heart.*" Or, stated more fully, one prays, "Immaculate Heart of Mary, keep me in your most pure heart, so that I may please Jesus through you, in you, and with you."[72] This part of Mother Teresa's consecration to Mary is the most profound. She's not just asking for Mary's heart to be in her but for her to be in Mary's heart! So, this is a prayer to love Jesus through Mary, in Mary, and with Mary. This is something more than simply having Mary lend us her heart. To understand and live it requires a loving dependence and profound union with Mary. The day after tomorrow, we'll cover what this means and how we get there. Tomorrow, we'll learn more about Mary's attitude of heart.

Today's Prayer:
> *Come, Holy Spirit, Living in Mary.*
> *Keep me in her most pure and Immaculate Heart.*

DAY 19
Heart-Pondering Prayer

Are you ready for your consecration to Mary? If not, then get ready! As I said in the beginning, after Consecration Day, everything changes. A gloriously new day dawns in our spiritual lives. Indeed, when we give Mary our "yes," she begins to arrange all the events and details of our lives in such beautiful, tender, and loving ways. So, we need to get ready. Specifically, we need to get ready to *recognize* the multitude of mercies that will come to us through her Spouse, the Holy Spirit.

Oftentimes, we don't recognize the many gifts that God pours out to us in our daily lives. What we do recognize are daily annoyances, burdens, difficulties, and inconveniences. These win our attention. These get us complaining. These get us in a bad mood and sap our energy. Wouldn't it be a tragedy if, after we started receiving even more gifts and graces through our consecration, we didn't change this negative attitude? Yes, it would be. So, we need to get ready, and Mother Teresa will help us.

Mother Teresa lived in some of the poorest environments on earth. She had to put up with burning heat, bad breath, stuffy rooms, nagging fatigue, endless responsibilities, bland food, hard beds, body odor, cold water bathing, and an agonizingly deep spiritual aridity. Yet, despite all this, she radiated joy. She smiled. She marveled at the good things God did in her life and in the lives of others, and she pondered the countless loving details arranged by Our Lady. Seeing and recognizing all this, she didn't complain.

How did Mother Teresa develop such a spiritual sensitivity and attitude of gratitude? What was her secret? Two things.

First, she followed the example of Mary who was always "pondering in her heart" the "good things" that God was doing in her life (see Luke 2:19, 51). Of course, like Mother Teresa, Mary also lived in poverty and surely bore her share of darkness in prayer. Yet she also found God in the details, pondered his goodness in her heart, and responded with praise: "*Magnificat!*" Indeed, she praised and thanked God in all things, because she found God in all things and pondered deeply in her heart his many signs of love.

Second, Mother Teresa followed the example of St. Ignatius of Loyola, the soldier saint and master of practical prayer. Specifically, she lived his method of making a daily examination of conscience ("examen"), whereby one reviews the day, at the end of the day, in the presence of the Lord. Contrary to what people often think about the examen, it's not simply a laundry list of sins. In fact, Ignatius directs people to spend most of their time reflecting not on sins but on the blessings of the day. It's really an exercise in recognizing the good things God is doing in our lives and how we are or are not responding to his love. It's an imitation of Mary's attitude of heart-pondering prayer. (To learn a method of making the examen, see this endnote.)[73]

God is always showering his love and mercy down on us in so many ways. It's important that we begin to recognize these blessings and thank him for them, especially because this shower of blessings is going to turn into a torrent of grace once we consecrate ourselves to Mary. So, let's get ready. Let's remember that, according to Mother Teresa, one important way that we live out our consecration is by recognizing God's blessings and pondering them, with Mary, deeply in our hearts. Such heart-pondering prayer leads to praise and thanks, and praise and thanks sets us on fire with divine love.

Today's Prayer:
> *Come, Holy Spirit, living in Mary.*
> *Help me to recognize and ponder in my heart all the good you do for me.*

DAY 20
A Consecration Covenant

Yesterday, I said we need to get ready for our consecration to Mary by learning to recognize all the blessings that will start pouring in. Today, we'll be shifting gears a bit. We'll be preparing for Consecration Day by reflecting on how serious a commitment Marian consecration really is. This is an important part of our preparation because the more seriously we take it, the more seriously the Mother of God will take it. Mother Teresa will be particularly helpful to us today; for she took her consecration to Mary very seriously.

Part of the reason Mother Teresa took her consecration so seriously has to do with her roots in Albanian culture. A key word in this culture is "*besa*." Literally translated, this means "faith," but its more complete meaning is "word of honor" and "to keep one's promise." Mother Teresa explains:

> [*Besa*] means even if you have killed my father and the police are after you, if I have given you my word, then even if the police kill me, still I will not disclose your name.[74]

In other words, to the mind of Mother Teresa, if you give your word to someone, you give yourself. Indeed, *besa* has a sacred character like a vow, oath, or covenant. Let's reflect on that last word, "covenant." This is how Mother Teresa described her consecration to Mary. It's a word that has rich, biblical meaning: It describes the bond of relationship between God and his people throughout salvation history. Such a bond is more than a contract, as scripture scholar, Scott Hahn, explains:

> [A] major difference between contracts and covenants may be discovered in their very distinctive forms of exchange. A contract is an exchange of property in the form of goods and services ("That is mine and this is yours"); whereas a covenant calls for the exchange of persons ("I am yours and you are mine"), creating a shared bond of interpersonal communion.[75]

Another feature of a covenant is that it usually entails certain rights and obligations. For example, in the marital covenant, a husband and wife have the right to enjoy one another in the spousal embrace of self-giving love, but they also have the obligation to care for and support one another "in good times and bad." Mother Teresa also understood her "Covenant of Consecration" with Mary as having certain rights and obligations, and she communicated this Marian spirituality to her religious family, the Missionaries of Charity.

Fr. Joseph Langford, MC, inspired by Mother Teresa's teaching on the Covenant of Consecration, spells out the details of a Missionary of Charity's rights and duties in her relationship with Mary, listing 12 corresponding rights and duties. The list begins, significantly, with Mary having the duty to give "her spirit and heart" and ends with each Missionary of Charity having the "right" to enter into Mary's heart and share her interior life. So, the two bookends of this covenant with Mary are Mother Teresa's two prayers that we learned about earlier: "Lend me your heart" and "keep me in your most pure heart." Everything in between is simply the terms of the relationship.

Let's conclude, then, by pondering the Missionaries of Charity's Consecration Covenant with Mary, beginning with its introductory paragraph:

Moved by an ardent desire to live in the closest union with you possible in this life, so as to more surely and fully arrive at union with your Son; I hereby pledge to live the spirit and terms of the following Covenant of Consecration as faithfully and generously as I am able.[76]

MARY'S DUTIES	MY DUTIES
1. To give of her spirit and heart.	1. Total gift of all I have and am.
2. To possess, protect, and transform me.	2. Total dependence on her.
3. To inspire, guide, and enlighten me.	3. Responsiveness to her spirit.
4. To share her experience of prayer and praise.	4. Faithfulness to prayer.
5. Responsibility for my sanctification.	5. Trust in her intercession.
6. Responsibility for all that befalls me.	6. Accept all as coming from her.
7. To share with me her virtues.	7. Imitate her spirit.
8. To provide for my spiritual and material needs.	8. Constant recourse to her.
9. Union with her heart.	9. Remembrance of her presence.
10. To purify me and my actions.	10. Purity of intention; self-denial.
11. Right to dispose of me, of my prayers and intercessions and graces.	11. Right to avail myself of her and her energies for the sake of the kingdom.
12. Total freedom in and around me, as she pleases in all things.	12. Right to enter into her heart, to share her interior life.

Today's Prayer:
> *Come, Holy Spirit, living in Mary.*
> *Help me to ardently make a Covenant of Consecration*
> *with Mary.*

'Be the One' (with Mary)

In case the list of 12 duties that we covered yesterday has got some of us feeling overwhelmed, today we'll focus on a simpler way of remembering the essence of Mother Teresa's consecration to Mary: "*Be the one.*" Or, more specifically, "Be the one, with Mary." What does this mean? The main clue comes from the Offertory verse (Ps 68:21) for the Mass of the Feast of the Sacred Heart:

> My heart had expected reproach and misery. And I looked for one that would grieve together with me, and there was none: and I sought one that would console me, and I found none.[77]

Mother Teresa responds, "Be the one." Be the one to console Jesus by satiating his burning thirst for love. She writes:

> Tell Jesus, "I will be the one." I will comfort, encourage and love Him. ... Be with Jesus. He prayed and prayed, and then He went to look for consolation, but there was none. ... I always write that sentence, "I looked for one to comfort Me, but I found no one." Then I write, "Be the one." So now you be that one. Try to be the one to share with Him, to comfort Him, to console Him. So let us ask Our Lady to help us understand.[78]

That last sentence is key. We need Our Lady to help us understand the thirst of Jesus. She's the one who consoles him best. She's the spouse of the Consoler, the Holy Spirit. Through Mary, the Holy Spirit can help us understand what it means to be a consoler of the Heart of Jesus:

[Let] us try in a special way to come as close as the
human heart can come to the Heart of Jesus and try
to understand as much as possible Jesus' terrible pain
caused to him by our sins and His Thirst for our
love. ... Thank God our Lady was there to understand
fully the thirst of Jesus for love. She must have
straight away said, "I satiate Your thirst with my love
and the suffering of my heart."[79]

Yes, we can thank God for Our Lady. She teaches us to "be
the one" with her, consoling Jesus on Calvary. She helps us to
"straight away" say, "Jesus, I satiate Your thirst." But what exactly
does this mean? What does it mean to satiate the thirst of Jesus?
Two things: to console Jesus the Head of his Mystical Body and
to console him in the members of his Body.

How do we console Jesus, the Head of the Body? By being
apostles of joy, which means "to console the Sacred Heart of
Jesus through joy," and we do this especially with Mary's joy. For
Mother Teresa continues, "Please ask our Lady to give me her
heart."[80] Mary is the one who, despite her own trial of darkness,
praises and thanks God in all things, smiles at him, and consoles
him with her love. It's simple and beautiful. Mother summarizes
it by her trademark three virtues: total surrender to God, loving
trust, and perfect cheerfulness. Basically, it's to be as a child, with
Mary, smiling at Jesus and loving him from the foot of the Cross.

Now, how do we console Jesus in the members of his Body?
By recognizing their thirst. Everyone thirsts: rich and poor,
young and old, believer and unbeliever. Everyone has a restless
heart for God, for man is a restless thirst. To console Jesus in
others is to respond to their suffering, especially to that deepest,
most universal suffering: the thirst for love. We should respond
to this thirst in others not with indifference but with a gentle
smile that says, "I delight that you exist, and I, too, understand
the pain of the thirst." Mother explains:

The greatest evil is the lack of love and charity, the
terrible indifference towards one's neighbor... .

[P]eople today are hungry for love, for understanding love which is much greater and which is the only answer to loneliness and great poverty."[81]

By accepting her own thirst (with Mary's help) and not running away from it, Mother Teresa could understand the thirst of others — both Jesus on the Cross and Jesus in her neighbor — and she became a true apostle of mercy and joy: a true missionary of charity.

Today's Prayer:
  Come, Holy Spirit, living in Mary.
    Help me to "be the one" to console Jesus with Mary.

Blessed John Paul II

During this fourth and final full week, we'll be focusing on the example and words of another great teacher of Marian consecration: Blessed John Paul II. "The most Marian Pope," as he's been called, profoundly deepened the Church's understanding of Marian consecration. Building on the work of the Second Vatican Council, he provides us with a thoroughly biblical treatment of Marian consecration — which he also calls "entrustment" — and homes in on the idea that it's Mary's role to lead us into the mystery of Christ's redeeming love and self-consecration to the Father.

DAY 22
Mary's Gift of Mercy

In 1917, while World War I raged, the Blessed Virgin Mary appeared to three shepherd children in Fatima, Portugal. She told them that the war would end but if people didn't convert, a worse war would follow and Russia would spread its errors throughout the world, causing more wars, martyrs, and persecutions of the Church. To prevent this, Mary asked that the Holy Father consecrate Russia to her Immaculate Heart and for people to make five consecutive "First Saturday" communions of reparation. In the end, she said, her Immaculate Heart would triumph.

It's interesting that Mary mentioned Russia. At the time, this was cause for confusion: Russia? Holy Russia? What errors would this devoutly Christian country spread throughout the world? And how could such a poor Russia exercise so much influence? (At this point in history, the Soviet revolution was in its infancy; the communist, atheist, totalitarian regime had not yet been established.)

After Mary gave her prophesy about Russia, the children saw a vision involving a "bishop dressed in white," who they understood to be the Pope. With great distress, they saw that he would suffer much and then be shot and killed. The children described what they saw only to Church authorities, who decided not to disclose it to the public. This became known as the last "secret" of Fatima.

Now, the very first apparition of Our Lady of Fatima happened on May 13, 1917, at 5 p.m. Exactly 64 years later, May 13, 1981, at 5 p.m., a small, open-air jeep rode out into St. Peter's Square, carrying Pope John Paul II, who warmly greeted pilgrims gathered in the square. At one point, the jeep stopped so the Pope could take a little girl into his arms. After he gave her back to her jubilant parents, the jeep continued on its way through the sea of waving, cheering pilgrims. Suddenly, a gunman fired two shots at the Pope from close range. The first bullet grazed his elbow. The second struck him in the abdomen and ricocheted inside him, shredding intestines and piercing his colon. Miraculously, the bullet missed the main abdominal artery by one tenth of an inch. Had it been struck or even grazed, John Paul would have bled to death on the way to the hospital. Realizing this blessing, the Pope stated that "One hand fired, and another guided the bullet."[82]

What hand guided the bullet? John Paul believes it was the hand of Our Lady of Fatima (the May 13th anniversary was not lost on him). In fact, after the shooting, he asked for the envelope containing the last secret of Fatima, the one about the "bishop dressed in white." Then, with Fatima much on his mind, he thought to consecrate the world to Mary's Immaculate Heart as soon as possible, and he began composing an act of entrustment, which he solemnly prayed less than a month later. Even before this, within a week of the shooting, he repeated his own personal consecration to Mary in a recorded address to the pilgrims gathered in St. Peter's Square: "To you, Mary, I repeat: *Totus tuus ego sum.*"[83]

On March 25, 1984, in St. Peter's Square, before the official statue of Our Lady of Fatima that had been flown in for the occasion, John Paul made a more solemn entrustment of the world to Mary's Immaculate Heart. He concluded the prayer with the following words:

Let there be revealed, once more, in the history of the world the infinite saving power of the redemption: the power of *merciful Love*! May it put a stop to evil!

May it transform consciences! May your Immaculate
Heart reveal for all the *light of Hope!*

After learning of the Pope's solemn entrustment, Sr. Lucia,
the lone survivor of the three Fatima seers, declared that it fully
satisfied Our Lady's original request. Five years later, the horrific,
Soviet, totalitarian regime that had terrorized millions of people
suddenly came to an end.

That victory won, the Pope didn't rest. What he once
called the "century of tears" was far from over. To confront the
ongoing evil and injustice in the world, he forcefully proclaimed,
with growing frequency, the saving power of God's *"merciful
Love."* His efforts to promote this message culminated in the
establishment of the universal Feast of Divine Mercy Sunday in
2000 and a solemn Act of Entrustment of the world to Divine
Mercy in 2002. Three years after this entrustment, the great
Marian Pope, the great Mercy Pope, died on a first Saturday and
the vigil of Divine Mercy Sunday. Mary had saved his life at the
dawn of his pontificate so that, through him, her divine Son
could lead the Church to the victory of Mercy and the triumph
of her Immaculate Heart.

Today's Prayer:
> *Come, Holy Spirit, living in Mary.*
> *Have mercy on us and on the whole world!*

DAY 23
Maternal Mediation

As one of our guides to Consecration Day, Blessed John
Paul II is a *triple gift.* Not only is he a Marian saint, like our other
three guides; not only is he brilliant and thoroughly trained in
theology, like de Montfort and Kolbe; but he is also a Pope.
Therefore, his words carry the teaching authority of the successor
of St. Peter … and the authoritative weight of an Ecumenical
Council! Well, this is true in the sense that his teachings on the
Mother of God are deeply rooted in the authoritative Mariology
of the Second Vatican Council. Because of this dependence on

the Council, before we look to John Paul's teaching on Marian consecration, let's see what the Council has to say about Mary. (Tomorrow, we'll begin to ponder how John Paul builds on Vatican II's teaching.)

One can find the main Marian teachings of Vatican II in the last chapter of the Dogmatic Constitution of the Church, known by its Latin title, *Lumen Gentium*. The heart of these teachings has to do with what's usually called Mary's "maternal mediation." Maternal mediation basically means that Mary is our spiritual mother (hence "maternal") who assists us from heaven with her prayers and motherly care to help bring us to God (hence "mediation"). While the term "maternal" should be familiar, "mediation" may need some explaining.

A mediator is someone who stands between two people for the sake of bringing them into unity. Thus, Jesus Christ is a mediator. He is the one who, after the Fall, stands between God and fallen humanity to bring us back into communion with God. And there's only one, as St. Paul makes clear, "[T]here is one mediator between God and men, the man Jesus Christ" (1 Tim 2:5).

If there's only one mediator between God and man, and if that one mediator is Jesus Christ, then why does the Second Vatican Council describe Mary as a mediator? Because God is generous. In other words, Jesus doesn't keep his role as mediator to himself. He wants Mary — and not just Mary, but all Christians — to share in his one mediation, though in subordinate ways. For instance, each of us shares in Christ's one mediation when we pray for one another "in Christ." I mentioned a similar point in the introduction when I wrote that God wants all of us to participate in his work of salvation. I also mentioned there that Mary has a uniquely important role in this work. Again, according to Vatican II, this special role is captured by the phrase "maternal mediation."

Among creatures, Mary's role in the ongoing work of salvation is by far the most important. She was given such an important role "not from some inner necessity" on God's part but "from the divine pleasure."[84] Again, we see God's generosity in including us in the work of redemption, we the very same creatures he came to redeem. The following passage from *Lumen Gentium* summarizes Mary's cooperation in this work both when she was on earth and now as she is in heaven:

> [T]he Blessed Virgin was on this earth the virgin Mother of the Redeemer, and above all others and in a singular way the generous associate and humble handmaid of the Lord. She conceived, brought forth, and nourished Christ. She presented him to the Father in the temple, and was united with him by compassion as he died on the cross. In this singular way she cooperated by her obedience, faith, hope, and burning charity in the work of our Savior in giving back supernatural life to souls. Wherefore she is our mother in the order of grace.
>
> This maternity of Mary in the order of grace began with the consent which she gave in faith at the annunciation and which she sustained without wavering beneath the cross, and lasts until the eternal fulfillment of all the elect. Taken up to heaven she did not lay aside this salvific duty, but by her constant intercession continued to bring us the gifts of eternal salvation. By her maternal charity, she cares for the brethren of her Son, who still journey on earth surrounded by dangers and difficulties, until they are led to the happiness of their true home. Therefore the Blessed Virgin is invoked by the Church under the titles of Advocate, Auxiliatrix, Adjutrix, and Mediatrix. This, however, is to be so understood that it neither takes away from nor adds anything to the dignity and efficaciousness of Christ the one Mediator.[85]

So, while on earth, Mary cooperated with God's plan of salvation "above all others," particularly by giving birth to and caring for Jesus. Now in heaven, Mary still cooperates in a special way in God's plan of salvation. Through her "constant intercession" and "maternal charity," she brings us grace, mercy, and the "gifts of eternal salvation." Tomorrow, we'll begin to see how John Paul develops this teaching on Mary's motherhood in the order of grace. For now, we can reflect on this great gift of God: Mary is our spiritual mother whose God-given task is to nurture us with tender care and the gifts and graces that come to us through her loving prayers.

Today's Prayer:
> *Come, Holy Spirit, living in Mary.*
> *Fill my heart with praise to God for giving me Mary as my spiritual mother.*

DAY 24
Mary's Retreat (Day One)

During this retreat, we've been pondering in our hearts certain truths of our faith that relate to Marian consecration. One might say we're on a kind of "pilgrimage of faith" leading up to Consecration Day. During her earthly life, Mary, too, was on a kind of retreat and pilgrimage of faith. She, too, pondered in her heart different truths related to Marian consecration. After all, she didn't discover all at once her vocation to be a spiritual mother and mediatrix. Like us, Mary needed to walk by faith while pondering in her heart. She, too, needed a time of preparation regarding her special role as our "mother in the order of grace."

Because Mary's maternal mediation is so central to a proper understanding of Marian consecration, we're going to spend the next few days making a retreat within our retreat. We'll do this by peering in on *Mary's retreat*. In other words, we're going to accompany Mary along the way that God led her to progressively discover her vocation to be our spiritual mother and mediatrix.

In some sense, Mary's retreat begins at the Annunciation. By her "yes" to God, her "*fiat*," she accepted her vocation to be the mother of Jesus. But did she also know that she was accepting the call to be the spiritual mother to all Christians as well? I don't know. What I do know is that the whole mystery of the Annunciation gave Mary something amazing to ponder, something that happens to be deeply related to Marian consecration and entrustment. Let me put it this way: Who was the first person to entrust himself to Mary? It wasn't St. Louis de Montfort. It was God the Father. John Paul explains, "For it must be recognized that before anyone else it was God himself, the Eternal Father, *who entrusted himself to the Virgin of Nazareth*, giving her his own Son in the mystery of the Incarnation."[86] Mary surely marveled at this act of humility on God's part. As she marveled and pondered it, might she have begun to have some inkling that God would later want the people he came to redeem to follow his example?

Mary had many other things to ponder during her preparation to be ever more completely our mother in the order of grace. The Synoptic Gospels (Matthew, Mark, and Luke) offer several points of reflection that speak to Mary's spiritual motherhood. Take, for example, the passage in the Gospel of Mark (3:31-35) where Mary and Jesus' cousins are outside, wanting to see Jesus, and so they send for him and call to him. Jesus responds by asking, "Who are my mother and my bretheren?" Then, looking at those sitting around him, he says "Here are my mother and my bretheren! Whoever does the will of God is my brother, and sister, and mother."

In giving this response, was Jesus being a bad son? No. He was being exactly the kind of son his Father wanted him to be. At the same time, he was preparing his mother for who he wanted her to be. Specifically, he was revealing to her the new filial bond of the kingdom that goes beyond the bonds of the flesh. In other words, he was pointing out the primacy of the spirit to the flesh, the primacy of the supernatural Fatherhood of God to the natural fatherhood (or motherhood) of man. It's likely that Mary immediately grasped some of what Jesus was trying to teach her. After all, for years she had pondered in her heart another strange response of Jesus, the one he gave when she found him in the Temple after three days of sorrowful searching: "Did you not know I must be about my Father's business?" (Lk 2:49).

During his public ministry, Jesus was indeed completely concerned with his Father's business. Now, a key part of this business involved preparing his mother for her new role in God's kingdom. Jesus knew that "in the dimension of the Kingdom of God and in the radius of the fatherhood of God" Mary's motherhood "takes on another meaning."[87] In the words reported by Mark that we read earlier, Jesus points to this meaning, "Whoever does the will of God is my brother, and sister, and mother." We can be sure that Mary pondered this in her heart and that she realized that by these words, Jesus was not rejecting her but rather preparing her.

Can we be sure Jesus wasn't rejecting Mary? Yes, we can. Even if Jesus' words sound like he's rejecting her, they aren't. In fact, if we consider a similar passage in the Gospel of Luke (11:27-28), it's clear that Jesus is actually *blessing* his mother. In this other passage, "a woman in the crowd raised her voice" and said to Jesus, "Blessed is the womb that bore you and the breasts that nursed you." Jesus responds in a way similar to what we read in Mark, "Blessed rather are those who hear the word of God and keep it." At first reading, this may seem like a rebuke of Mary. But it's not. After all, who heard the word of God and kept it better than Mary? Nobody. Thus, Jesus is actually blessing his mother, and she would have realized it.

Mary is an incredibly perceptive woman, and she paid close attention to Jesus' every word and action. The subtleties of his teaching were not lost on her, and she progressively came to realize the unfolding mystery of her own unique motherhood:

> [A]s the messianic mission of her Son grew clearer to her eyes and spirit, [Mary] herself as a mother became ever more open to *that new dimension of motherhood* which was to constitute her "part" beside her Son. Had she not said from the very beginning: "Behold, I am the handmaid of the Lord; let it be to me according to your word" (Lk 1:38)? Through faith Mary continued to hear and to ponder that word ... . Thus in a sense Mary as

Mother became *the first "disciple" of her Son*, the first
to whom he seemed to say: "Follow me" … .[88]

What a joy it must have been for Jesus to have *one disciple*
who fully understood him. What a consolation to his Heart to
find such attentiveness to God's Word!

Tomorrow, we'll reflect more on Mary's attentiveness and
how it led her to discover yet another aspect to her "part" beside
her son in his work of salvation. This part does indeed involve,
as John Paul wrote, a "new dimension of her motherhood."
Thus, at Cana, we'll see that she gives *birth* to the faith of Jesus'
disciples by initiating his first miracle, which comes through her
motherly attentiveness to human need.

Today's Prayer:
> *Come, Holy Spirit, living in Mary.*
> *Help me to be faithful to heart-pondering prayer,*
> *as was Mary.*

DAY 25
Mary's Retreat (Day Two)

Yesterday, we began a "retreat within our retreat" by joining
Mary's retreat. In other words, we began to ponder the ways
that Jesus prepared Mary to understand and fully embrace her
new motherly role in the kingdom of God. Today, we continue
this retreat at the wedding feast of Cana, where Mary's
motherly mediation gloriously shines forth. Let's review the
scene (Jn 2:1-12).

The mother of Jesus is at a wedding feast, and Jesus and his
disciples are also invited — presumably because of Mary. The
wine runs short. Mary notices this, and brings it to the attention
of her Son, "They have no wine." Jesus seems to rebuke her,
"Woman, what have you to do with me? My hour has not yet
come." Mary nevertheless tells the servants, "Do whatever he
tells you." The servants follow Jesus' orders to fill stone jars with
water. Then the water becomes wine, and the disciples believe.

Let's now ponder deeply John Paul's commentary on this

scene. His words get to the heart of Mary's role in our lives and explain why we should be seeking to consecrate ourselves to her:

[Cana] clearly outlines *the new dimension*, the new meaning *of Mary's motherhood*. ... [It is] a new kind of motherhood according to the spirit and not just according to the flesh, that is to say *Mary's solicitude for human beings*, her coming to them in the wide variety of their wants and needs. At Cana in Galilee there is shown only one concrete aspect of human need, apparently a small one of little importance ("They have no wine"). But it has a symbolic value: this coming to the aid of human needs means, at the same time, bringing those needs within the radius of Christ's messianic mission and salvific power. Thus there is a mediation: Mary places herself between her Son and mankind in the reality of their wants, needs, and sufferings. *She puts herself "in the middle,"* that is to say *she acts as a mediatrix not as an outsider, but in her position as Mother*. She knows that as such she can point out to her Son the needs of mankind, and in fact, she "has the right" to do so. Her mediation is thus in the nature of intercession: Mary "intercedes" for mankind. And that is not all. As a Mother she also *wishes the messianic power of her Son to be manifested*, that salvific power of his which is meant to help man in his misfortunes, to free him from the evil which in various forms and degrees weighs heavily upon his life.

... Another essential element of Mary's maternal task is found in her words to the servants: "Do whatever he tells you." *The Mother* of Christ presents herself as the *spokeswoman of her Son's will*, pointing out those things which must be done so that the salvific power of the Messiah may be manifested. At Cana, thanks to the intercession of Mary and the obedience of the servants, Jesus begins "his hour." At Cana Mary appears as believing in Jesus. Her faith evokes his first "sign" and helps to kindle the faith of the disciples.

... [T]he episode at Cana in Galilee offers us *a sort of first announcement of Mary's mediation*, wholly oriented toward Christ and tending to the revelation of his salvific power.[89]

I'd like to highlight a few important points from this passage for us to ponder. (1) Not by necessity but by God's choice, "the handmaid of the Lord" who does the Father's will perfectly has a "right" as mother and mediatrix to point out to her Son the needs of mankind. Shouldn't we have recourse to such a powerful Mother of Mercy with regard to our own needs and intentions? (2) Mary needs servants who will obey her words, "Do whatever he tells you." Are we ready to be her servants so Jesus can begin his "hour" in our day? (3) It's clear from the words "Do whatever he tells you" that Mary's role is "wholly oriented toward Christ" and tends to the revelation of his saving power. Mary's mediation, therefore, is in union with and subordinate to the one mediation of Jesus Christ, our Savior.

Today's Prayer:
> *Come, Holy Spirit, living in Mary.*
> *Remind me to ask for Mary's powerful intercession in my times of need.*

DAY 26
Mary's Retreat (Day Three)

Yesterday, at the wedding feast of Cana, we saw a glorious example of Mary's motherly mediation. After this event, Mary surely pondered it deeply in her heart and discovered much about her maternal mediation. Yet Cana was not the most important part of her preparation. The "crowning moment" of her preparation — indeed, its full actualization — came at Calvary.

At Calvary, Mary suffers with Christ. Through faith, she is "perfectly united with Christ in his self-emptying." Through faith, she shares in the whole "shocking mystery" of his gift of himself out of love for us. Through faith, "the Mother shares in the death of her Son, in his redeeming death."[90] Before his death, Jesus has one more lesson for his perfect disciple, who has followed him to the Cross and fully accepted to suffer with him. Seeing her standing at the foot of the Cross next to his beloved disciple, John, he says, "Woman, behold, your son." Then, to John, "Behold, your mother" (Jn 19:26-27). With these words, Jesus gives Mary as Mother "to every single individual and all mankind."[91]

According to John Paul, this "new motherhood of Mary" is "*the fruit of the 'new' love* which came to definitive maturity in her at the foot of the Cross, through her sharing in the redemptive love of her son."[92] This "new love," says John Paul, actually causes a "transformation" in Mary's motherhood such that she burns even more with love for all those for whom Jesus suffered and died.

This idea that Mary, at the foot of the Cross, received a new, burning love for souls may remind us of Mother Teresa's deep insight about Mary. Recall that, for Teresa, Mary is the one who took Jesus' words "I thirst" most deeply to heart and that she helps others to take them to heart as well. Anyway, John Paul further reflects on Mary's transformation in love:

> [A]t the foot of the Cross there was … accomplished her maternal *cooperation* with the Savior's whole mission through her actions and sufferings. Along the path of this collaboration with the work of her Son, the Redeemer, Mary's motherhood itself underwent a singular transformation, becoming even more imbued with "burning charity" toward all those to whom Christ's mission was directed. Through this "burning charity," which sought to achieve, in union with Christ, the restoration of "supernatural life to souls," Mary *entered, in a way all her own, into the one mediation* "between God and men" *which is the mediation of the man Christ Jesus.*[93]

At Calvary, Mary's preparation is ended. She has received the full gift of her universal spiritual motherhood and mediation, which is a unique cooperation in Christ's work of redemption and a sharing in his mediation.

After Jesus' death on the Cross, we don't hear about Mary exercising her new motherhood until the day before Pentecost, when the apostles, together with "the women and Mary the mother of Jesus and his brethren" (Acts 1:14), are devoting themselves to prayer in the upper room. John Paul comments, "We see Mary prayerfully imploring the gift of the Spirit, who had already overshadowed her at the Annunciation."[94] He goes on to point out that Mary is the "discreet yet essential presence" that indicates the path of "birth from the Holy Spirit" first at the Annunciation and now at the birth of the Church.

Mary's new spiritual motherhood is deeply connected with the Church, "*with maternal love she cooperates in the birth and development* of the sons and daughters of Mother Church."[95] This birth and development has its source in the Church's sacramental life, where Mary's motherly mediation is particularly present. For instance, Mary is surely interceding and active with her Spouse, the Holy Spirit, when the Spirit transforms us into members of Christ's body at Baptism. Moreover, she is just as present and active with her Spouse at Mass; for it is at Mass that Christ's "*true body born of the Virgin Mary*" becomes present.[96] Because of the centrality of the Eucharist in Christian faith and life, Mary is always striving to lead the faithful to it.

As we close today's reflection, which concludes the three days of "Mary's spiritual motherhood retreat," we should keep in mind one important point: Mary's new motherhood is not some vague or abstract sort of thing. It's concrete and personal. And even though it's universal, it's also intensely particular. Mary is *your* mother. She is *my* mother. In this light, John Paul thinks it's significant that Mary's new motherhood on Calvary is expressed in the singular, "Behold, your son" *not* "Behold, your billions of spiritual children." The Pope gets to the heart of it when he says, "Even when the same woman is the mother of many children, her personal relationship with each one of them is of the very essence of motherhood."[97] In short: Mary is uniquely, particularly, personally your mother and my mother, and she doesn't lose us in the crowd.

Today's Prayer:
> *Come, Holy Spirit, living in Mary.*
> *Thank you for the gift of my loving Mother, Mary.*

Marian Entrustment (Part One)

Now that we've completed our three-day, mini-retreat with Mary, we should have a clearer sense of Mary's maternal mediation. This motherly mediation is the key that unlocks the whole theology of Marian consecration. And now that we have this key, we're ready to learn exactly what John Paul means by Marian consecration, or as he usually refers to it, "Marian entrustment." To begin, we need to go back to the foot of the Cross.

"Woman, behold, your son." With these words, Jesus is entrusting all of humanity to Mary's motherly care. He's making her the spiritual mother of all. And as we learned yesterday, Mary fully accepted this gift "with burning love."

Next, Jesus speaks to John, the beloved disciple, who represents all of us: "Behold, your mother." Jesus is now giving us a gift, the great gift of his mother as our spiritual mother. Do we accept this gift? Yes. At least we're trying to (otherwise, we wouldn't be making this retreat). But how do we accept it? This is the crucial question.

According to Pope John Paul, the following Gospel text tells us how we are to accept Mary as our spiritual mother, "And from that hour the disciple took her to his own home" (Jn 19:27). The Pope describes this action with one word: "entrusting." We see an example of this in the person of John, who entrusted himself to Mary, who was herself entrusted to John by Christ, "Behold, your mother." John's entrusting of himself to Mary is *his response to Christ's command from the Cross*, but it's not only that. It's also *a response to Mary's "burning love" for us:* "entrusting is *the response* to a person's love, and in particular *to the love of a mother*." John Paul goes on to describe the nature of this entrusting of oneself to Mary:

Entrusting himself to Mary in a filial manner, the Christian, like the Apostle John, "welcomes" the Mother of Christ "into his own home" and brings her into everything that makes up his inner life, that is to say into his human and Christian "I": he *took her to his own home.*" Thus the Christian seeks to be taken into that "maternal charity" with which the Redeemer's Mother "cares for the brethren of her Son," "in whose birth and development she cooperates" in the measure of the gift proper to each one through the power of Christ's Spirit. Thus also is exercised that motherhood in the Spirit which became Mary's role at the foot of the Cross and in the Upper Room.[98]

This entrusting of oneself to Mary, which the Pope beautifully describes as taking her "into one's own home," should be understood as our following of Christ's own example — he first entrusted himself to Mary at the Annunciation and then throughout the Hidden Life — and as his will for his disciples. After all, he himself initiates such entrustment, "Behold, your mother." But why does Christ do this? Is it that he wants to distance himself from us? No. He's bringing us closer to himself by giving us to the one who is closest to him, the same one who directs everything to him, "Do whatever he tells you."

Mary wants to act upon all those who entrust themselves to her as children. "And it is well known," says the Pope, "that the more her children persevere and progress in this attitude, the nearer Mary leads them to the 'unsearchable riches of Christ.'"[99] Again, this is so both because of the unique closeness of Mary to Christ and because of her special role of bringing others into the intimacy she shares with him.

Tomorrow, we'll see how this closeness of Mary to Christ, particularly in his consecration of himself for our sake, helps us make our own consecration to Christ. This is the whole purpose behind why we entrust ourselves to Mary: It's so she can bring us even closer to Christ through her powerful prayers and motherly love.

Today's Prayer:
> *Come, Holy Spirit, living in Mary.*
> *Prepare me to entrust myself completely to Mary so she*
> *can bring me closer to Christ.*

DAY 28
Marian Entrustment (Part Two)

Let's return to Fatima, where we started this week — but this time let's go with Blessed John Paul II.

Exactly one year after being shot in St. Peter's Square, John Paul went to Fatima "in order to give thanks that the mercy of God and the protection of the Mother of Christ" had saved his life.[100] On that occasion, he delivered a heartfelt homily that's a rich source of the theology of Marian consecration and entrustment. The entire homily and Act of Entrustment are too long to cite here. So, I'm going to summarize. Specifically, I'm going to draw out from them the connection the Pope makes between consecration to Mary, Divine Mercy, and the redeeming consecration of Christ. Let's start with the connection between Mary and Divine Mercy.

Before we begin, a few things about Divine Mercy: (1) According to John Paul, Divine Mercy is the limit imposed by God on evil, the love of God in the face of evil; (2) Divine Mercy is symbolized by the pierced side of Christ and the blood and water that gushed forth from his side; (3) a central part of the modern Divine Mercy devotion is the Chaplet of Divine Mercy, which offers atonement and implores mercy for our sins and those of the whole world. In what follows, notice how these three aspects of Divine Mercy are central to the Pope's most important homily on Marian consecration.

The homily's context is the widespread, "almost apocalyptic" evil of our time, an evil that "menaces," that is "spreading," and that gathers "like a dark cloud over mankind." The Pope confesses that this evil causes "trepidation" in his heart. Despite this, he finds hope in "a Love more powerful than evil" which no "sin of the world can ever overcome." This Love he identifies as "merciful Love."[101]

And what about this *merciful Love?* What does it have to do with Marian consecration? Everything. It has everything to do with consecration because Mary is the one who brings us to the source of merciful Love. Mary is the one who brings us to the love that is more powerful than evil. Indeed, as John Paul says in his homily, consecration to the Immaculate Heart means "drawing near, through the Mother's intercession, to the very Fountain of Life that sprang from Golgotha."[102] What is this fountain of life? The Pope identifies it as "the Fountain of Mercy."[103] It's the pierced side of Christ from which blood and water flowed as a source of grace and mercy. And it's through this wound in Christ's Heart that "reparation is made continually for the sins of the world." Moreover, through this Fountain of Mercy, we find "a ceaseless source of new life and holiness."[104]

The Pope goes on to explain that consecration to the Immaculate Heart of Mary means "returning to the Cross of the Son." It means bringing the world and all its problems and sufferings to "the pierced Heart of the Savior" and thus "back to the very source of its Redemption." It means bringing the world, through Mary, to Divine Mercy! The power of the Redemption, the power of merciful Love, "is always greater than man's sin and the 'sin of the world'" and is "infinitely superior to the whole range of evil in man and the world."

Now, Mary knows the power of the Redemption, the power of merciful Love, better than anyone. In fact, John Paul says she knows it "more than any other heart in the whole universe, visible and invisible." Therefore, she calls us not only to conversion but "to accept her motherly help to return to the source of Redemption." For again, Mary's task is to bring us to the Fountain of Mercy, to the pierced side of Christ, to his Merciful Heart.

Essentially, then, consecrating ourselves to Mary "means accepting her help to offer ourselves and the whole of mankind"[105] to the infinitely Holy God. It means entrusting ourselves to she who was most united to Christ's own consecration: "Hail to you who are wholly united to the redeeming consecration of your Son!"[106] It means entrusting ourselves to Mary's prayers, that she may "help us to live with the whole truth of the consecration of Christ for the entire human family of the modern world."[107] In other words, consecrating ourselves to Mary means relying on her motherly intercession to help us offer ourselves more fully to Christ in his own consecration for our redemption.

After putting himself and the world into Mary's hands and Heart, after giving himself to she who is most wholly united to Jesus' consecration, the Pope prays the heart of his act of entrustment. Let's conclude by pondering it deeply in our own hearts:

> "For God so loved the world that he gave his only Son, that whoever believes in him should not perish but have eternal life" (Jn 3:16).
>
> It was precisely by reason of this love that the Son of God consecrated himself for all mankind: "And for their sake I consecrate myself, that they also may be consecrated in truth" (Jn 17:19).
>
> By reason of that consecration the disciples of all ages are called to spend themselves for the salvation of the world, and to supplement Christ's afflictions for the sake of his body, that is the Church (see 2 Cor 12:15; Col 1:24).
>
> Before you, Mother of Christ, before your Immaculate Heart, I today, together with the whole Church, unite myself with our Redeemer in this his consecration for the world and for people, which only in his divine Heart has the power to obtain pardon and to secure reparation.[108]

Today's Prayer:
Come, Holy Spirit, living in Mary.
>*Draw me in, with, and through Mary to the Fountain of Love and Mercy.*

FINAL FIVE DAYS
Synthesis and Review

For four weeks, we've been reflecting on what Marian consecration is all about — and we've covered a lot of material. While our prayer program of daily pondering the text has helped us digest some of the information, we can still go deeper. To do this, we need what Pope John Paul calls Mary's "wise capacity for remembering and embracing in a single gaze of faith." [109] *We can develop this "wise capacity" by continuing what we've been doing all along, namely, pondering in our hearts (see Lk 2:19), but now with a more refined focus.*

To give us this more refined focus, for each week of the retreat, I've chosen three words that summarize a given week's teaching. So, over the next four days, we'll reflect on three words each day, pondering their meaning for Marian consecration. I'm confident that if we dedicate ourselves to this more refined prayer pondering, we'll be able to embrace the truth of Marian consecration "in a single gaze of faith." After these four days of review, we'll find a synthesis of what we've learned in a single formula of consecration that aims to capture the essence of Marian consecration.

St. Louis de Montfort

Three words summarize what we learned from St. Louis de Montfort: (1) Passion, (2) Baptism, and (3) Gift. Let's ponder each one in turn.

PASSION

Recall that St. Louis inherited his father's fiery temper. This could have led to disaster, but Louis consecrated himself to Jesus through Mary. He allowed Mary to take charge of his life and to do with him as she willed. And what did Mary do with him? She set him on fire. She transformed his unholy anger into a blazing holy fire. She acted with her Spouse, the Holy Spirit, to fill Louis with passion and zeal for Christ, and he proceeded to set all of Brittany on fire with a love for Jesus the Incarnate Wisdom — and not only Brittany. De Montfort's inspiring teaching blazed through the centuries, igniting saints, popes, and even poor sinners with a burning love for God.

We may not have been born with St. Louis's fiery temper, but we could all use a portion of his zealous spirit. We could all use a greater outpouring of the Holy Spirit, who stirs souls into flame and fills them with holy fire. How do we invite this fire? How do we call it down? By imitating de Montfort's example of going to Mary, depending on Mary, and being with Mary. For, as Louis himself says, when the Holy Spirit, Mary's spouse, finds a soul united to Mary, "He flies there. He enters there in His fullness; He communicates Himself to that soul abundantly, and to the full extent to which it makes room for His spouse."[110] The Holy Spirit wants to work his wonders even in our day. He wants to raise up new saints, great saints. Why, then, does he do so, so rarely? According to de Montfort, it's because he rarely finds in us a sufficiently great union with Mary.

In this final stretch that leads to Consecration Day, may we go with great zeal to give ourselves completely to Mary and allow the Holy Spirit to fly to us and fill us with holy passion and fire.

BAPTISM

Saint Louis places his devotion to Mary squarely within the mystery of Christ. The best example of this is how he begins his formula for consecration with a renewal of baptismal vows; for Baptism is all about Christ. At Baptism, we're transformed into members of the Body of Christ, made into "other Christs."

Baptism also has to do with the Holy Spirit. I say this because it was the Holy Spirit who first formed Christ, and it is the Holy Spirit who continues to form other Christs — the members of Christ's Body — at every Baptism.

Now, who does the Holy Spirit use to form Christ? He uses Mary, even though he has no absolute need of her. So, for example, he made use of Mary at the Annunciation, which led to the birth of Jesus Christ our Savior. He made use of Mary just before Pentecost, which led to the birth of the Body of Christ, the Church. He makes use of Mary at every Baptism, which gives birth to "other Christs," the members of his Body. The Holy Spirit always makes use of Mary to give birth to Christ! And the more he finds a soul that is united to Mary "the more active and mighty He becomes in producing Jesus Christ in that soul, and that soul in Jesus Christ."[111]

It is fitting, then, that de Montfort has us renew our baptismal promises in the context of giving ourselves to Mary. For it is her job, with the Holy Spirit, to bring the grace of Baptism to its fulfillment. Baptism isn't the end; it's a marvelous beginning, a gloriously new morning. Yes, it transforms us, making us into members of Christ's Body — but there's more work to be done. Baptism is an already-but-not-yet reality. It already makes us into Christ (as a member of his Body) but not yet fully formed in Christ. After Baptism, we still have to grow in Christ, and it's Mary's job to oversee and nurture this growth, with the Spirit. Thus, there's no question of de Montfort's devotion to Mary "taking us away from Christ."[112] Mary's whole goal is to lead us to Christ and to bring us to the point where we can say with St. Paul, "It is no longer I that live but Christ" (Gal 2:20). *The whole goal of true devotion to Mary is our ongoing, post-baptismal transformation in Christ.*

GIFT

If only we have the courage to give ourselves completely to Mary, then we'll experience Marian consecration as an incredible gift. Moreover, the more we give ourselves to her, the more we'll experience the greatness of this gift.

We give, and she gives back infinitely more. We give her our sinful selves, and she gives us her Immaculate Heart. We give her our own meager merits, and she not only augments and purifies them with her perfect love but gives us her infinitely greater merits and graces. We become empty after having given her all, and she fills us with the Spirit of God. She cares for our family, friends, and loved ones on our behalf — even better than we ourselves can. She anticipates our needs and orders every detail of our lives for the greater glory of God. The path of holiness with her is "a path of roses and honey" compared to walking it without being consecrated to her. Indeed, she makes even our crosses and trials into something sweet. Moreover, she protects us from temptation and the attacks of the evil one.

Belonging completely to Mary is the quickest, easiest, and surest way to Jesus. If we were to fully realize how great a gift consecration to Jesus through Mary is, we'd almost never stop smiling and praising God for giving it.

Today's prayer:
Spend the day pondering de Montfort's Marian teaching as it is summarized by these three words: Passion, Baptism, and Gift.

DAY 30
St. Maximilian Kolbe

Three words summarize what we learned from St. Maximilian Kolbe: (1) Mystery, (2) Militia, and (3) Love. Let's ponder each one in turn.

MYSTERY

Who are you, O Immaculate Conception? St. Maximilian gives us the key to this mystery: The Holy Spirit is the *uncreated* Immaculate Conception, and Mary is the *created* Immaculate Conception. She is perfectly united to the Holy Spirit, because she was conceived without sin, never sinned, and always does the will of God perfectly. She allows the Holy Spirit to overshadow her, take possession of her soul, and bear fruit through her. The Holy Spirit delights in always working in and through Mary to save all the other creatures made in God's image, first by bringing about the Incarnation in her womb and then by making use of her to form the image of her Son in all of the baptized. While Kolbe gives us the key to the mystery, he doesn't fully unlock it. Rather, he invites us to ponder ever more deeply the relationship between Mary and the Holy Spirit, a relationship that goes even deeper than that of marriage.

MILITIA

The name "Maximilian" means "the greatest." Saint Maximilian Kolbe was given this name because his superiors recognized his immense natural and spiritual gifts. He accepted it because it corresponded to his heart of hearts: "I don't just want to give God great glory but the *greatest* glory."

Kolbe recognized that the greatest way to give glory to God is to unite oneself to the creature who glorifies God most perfectly, Mary Immaculate. He also realized that the way to give God the greatest glory is not to do so just as one person, but to have a whole army ("Militia") of people who give God the greatest glory. In fact, he wanted this army of the Immaculate ("Militia Immaculata") to eventually get the whole world to give God the greatest glory, through her, and as soon as possible.

While the goal of Kolbe's program is the conversion of the whole world, it begins with oneself. One must first give himself completely to the Immaculata as her possession and property and stay in union with her and totally dependent on her. Then, one is to inspire others to give themselves to her and to live in total dependence on her, so she can use them as consecrated instruments to bring the whole world to the Merciful Heart of Jesus.

"Through the Immaculata we will attain the ultimate purpose of the [Militia Immaculata], that is, the greatest possible glory to God."[113]

LOVE

Kolbe was united to Mary through a dependence of love. He tells us that we also ought to love the Immaculata. How? *By relying on her powerful intercession, experiencing her tender care, speaking to her from our hearts, letting ourselves be led by her, having recourse to her in all things, and trusting her completely.* Recall his words, "My dear, dear brothers, our dear little, little mother, the Immaculate Mary, can do anything for us. We are her children. Turn to her. She will overcome everything."[114]

When we experience Mary's tender care for us, we'll fall more in love with her. But we have to speak with her. We have to ask her. Yet what if, even after many signs of her love and care, we still don't feel love for the Immaculata or her love for us? Kolbe explains:

> Never worry that you do not feel this love. If you have the will to love, you already give a proof that you love. What counts is the will to love. External feeling is also a fruit of grace, but it does not always follow the will. Sometimes, my dear ones, the thought, a sad longing, as if a plea or a complaint, may occur to you: "Does the Immaculata still love me?" Most beloved children! I tell you all and each one individually, in her name (mark that: in her name!), she loves every one of you. She loves you very much and at every moment with no exception. This ... I repeat for you in her name.[115]

Today's Prayer:
> *Spend the day pondering Kolbe's Marian teaching as it is summarized by these three words: Mystery, Militia, and Love.*

DAY 31
Blessed Mother Teresa

Three words summarize what we learned from Blessed Mother Teresa: (1) Thirst, (2) Heart, and (3) Covenant. Let's ponder each one in turn.

THIRST

> ... [Our Lady] was the first person to hear Jesus' cry "I Thirst" with St. John, and I am sure Mary Magdalen. Because Our Lady was there on Calvary, she knows how real, how deep is His longing for you and for the poor. Do we know? Do we feel as she? Ask her to teach ... . Her role is to bring you face to face, as John and Magdalen, with the love in the Heart of

Jesus crucified. Before it was Our Lady pleading with Mother, now it is Mother in her name pleading with you —"listen to Jesus' thirst."

Let us try in a special way to come as close as the human heart can come to the Heart of Jesus and try to understand as much as possible Jesus' terrible pain caused to him by our sins and His Thirst for our love. Thank God our Lady was there to understand fully the thirst of Jesus for love. She must have straight away said, "I satiate Your thirst with my love and the suffering of my heart."

So let us ask Our Lady to help us understand.

HEART

A key to Mother Teresa's understanding of consecration is "heart," specifically, the Immaculate Heart. Recall her two prayers to Mary, "Lend me your heart" and "Keep me in your most pure heart." Also, recall the importance of our imitating Mary's pondering heart. Let's start with the two prayers and then review Mary's heart-pondering attitude.

Lend me your heart. By this prayer, Mother Teresa was asking Our Lady to give her the love of her heart. In other words, she says "Mary, help me to love with the perfect love of your Immaculate Heart." Remember, Mother Teresa's passionate desire was to satiate the thirst of Jesus for love, and she wanted to do this in the best possible way. What better way to love Jesus than with the perfect, humble, immaculate heart of his mother? Here, Mother Teresa found the secret to living out her vocation to the full: "Mary, lend me your Immaculate Heart."

Keep me in your most pure heart. Or, stated more fully, one prays, "Immaculate Heart of Mary, keep me in your most pure heart, so that I may please Jesus through you, in you, and with you."[116] This part of Mother Teresa's consecration to Mary is the most profound. She's not just asking for Mary's heart to be in her but for her to be in Mary's heart! So, this is a prayer to love Jesus through Mary, in Mary, and with Mary. This is something more than simply having Mary lend us her heart. To understand this and live it requires a loving dependence and profound union with Mary. This is expressed more fully in the next section "covenant."

Pondering heart. Mother Teresa developed an "attitude of gratitude" by following the example of Mary who was always "pondering in her heart" the "good things" that God was doing in her life (see Luke 2:19, 51). Specifically, Mother Teresa followed this example through her fidelity to the examination of conscience. In other words, at the end of each day, she would ponder in her heart all the good things God had done for her that day and would reflect on how she was or was not fully responding to his love.

COVENANT

Moved by an ardent desire to live in the closest union with you [Mary] possible in this life, so as to more surely and fully arrive at union with your Son; I hereby pledge to live the spirit and terms of the following Covenant of Consecration as faithfully and generously as I am able.

MARY'S DUTIES	MY DUTIES
1. To give of her spirit and heart.	1. Total gift of all I have and am.
2. To possess, protect, and transform me.	2. Total dependence on her.
3. To inspire, guide, and enlighten me.	3. Responsiveness to her spirit.
4. To share her experience of prayer and praise.	4. Faithfulness to prayer.
5. Responsibility for my sanctification.	5. Trust in her intercession.
6. Responsibility for all that befalls me.	6. Accept all as coming from her.
7. To share with me her virtues.	7. Imitate her spirit.
8. To provide for my spiritual and material needs.	8. Constant recourse to her.
9. Union with her heart.	9. Remembrance of her presence.
10. To purify me and my actions.	10. Purity of intention; self-denial.
11. Right to dispose of me, of my prayers and intercessions and graces.	11. Right to avail myself of her and her energies for the sake of the kingdom.
12. Total freedom in and around me, as she pleases in all things.	12. Right to enter into her heart, to share her interior life.

Today's Prayer:
Spend the day pondering Teresa's Marian teaching as it is summarized by these three words: Thirst, Heart, and Covenant.

DAY 32
Blessed John Paul II

Three words summarize what we learned from Blessed John Paul II: (1) Mother, (2) "Entrust-acration," and (3) Mercy. Let's ponder each one in turn.

MOTHER

John Paul's teaching on Marian consecration not only carries with it his authority as Pope but also the authoritative weight of an Ecumenical Council, because he repeats and deepens Vatican II's teaching on Mary. Therefore, his teaching actually constitutes the mind and heart of the Church today, and we should pay particular attention to it. So what is the mind and heart of the Church telling us about Mary? It's pointing to Mary's maternal mediation. It's saying she's our mother in the order of grace. It's proclaiming the Good News that God has given us a spiritual mother who prayerfully, lovingly attends to our growth in grace and holiness. This new motherhood of Mary in the life of the Church, in the life of each of one of us, is the constant, consoling, beautiful background to everything we've said about Marian consecration — or what John Paul often calls "entrustment."

ENTRUST-ACRATION

Seeing Mary standing at the foot of the Cross next to his beloved disciple, John, Jesus said, "Woman, behold, your son." Then, to John, "Behold, your mother" (Jn 19:26-27). These words summarize what we already covered in the last point, that Mary is our spiritual mother. But then we read the next verse, "Then the disciple took her into his home." Here is the heart of our response to Jesus entrusting us to Mary as our mother: We are to then entrust ourselves to her by taking her "into our homes." In other words, we're to take her into our inner life, into all that concerns us. We are to let her into our joys and sorrows, hopes and fears, plans and activities.

When we let Mary into our lives, when we entrust ourselves to her care, she intercedes for us, consoles us, and gives us courage and strength to unite ourselves more fully to Jesus' own consecration of himself for the life of the world. In other words, she brings us to the Cross of Jesus, which is the final meaning of Jesus' self-consecration, and she inspires us to spend ourselves for the salvation of the world, to take up our part in the work of redemption. As we take up our cross, as we live within Christ's own consecration, we may become spiritually thirsty, desolate, and tired. That's when Mary carries us to the pierced side of Christ, the Fountain of Mercy, where we find a ceaseless source of strength and holiness.

Thus, to John Paul's mind, entrustment to Mary leads to our consecration to Christ. In other words, one might say it's a movement of "entrust-acration."

MERCY

Ultimately, Marian consecration leads us to Divine Mercy. Acts of consecration to the Immaculate Heart of Mary lead to acts of trust in the Merciful Heart of Jesus. We see this in the story of Fatima and Pope John Paul, and especially in the Pope's homily during his pilgrimage to Fatima in 1982, a pilgrimage of thanksgiving "to the mercy of God ... and the Mother of Christ" for having saved his life.

In that homily, John Paul repeatedly pointed out how Marian consecration leads us to the pierced Heart of Jesus, the Fountain of Mercy. This connection is part of the will of Jesus himself, who said to Sr. Lucia in 1936 that he wills the consecration to Mary's Heart "because I want my whole Church to acknowledge that consecration [that my mother requested at Fatima] as a triumph of the Immaculate Heart of Mary, so that it may extend its veneration later on, and put the devotion to this Immaculate Heart beside the devotion to My Sacred Heart."[117] Jesus wants to extend veneration and devotion to the Immaculate Heart of Mary because she leads us most perfectly to him and helps us to receive the infinite mercy of his Heart.

Today's Prayer:

Spend the day pondering John Paul's Marian teaching as it is summarized by these three words: Mother, Entrust-acration, and Mercy.

DAY 33
Putting It All Together

For the last four days, we've been reviewing the last four weeks of our retreat. During these days, we've not only been reviewing the material, we've also begun to put together all that we've learned. I say we've *begun* to put it together. We're probably not yet at a point where we can grasp the manifold truth of Marian consecration "in a single gaze," as John Paul put it. To get to this point, a unifying statement may be helpful, something like the "First Principle and Foundation" that St. Ignatius of Loyola came up with to summarize and give clarity and focus to his spirituality.

Actually, I think we need more than just a statement. We need a prayer, something we can frequently repeat, even everyday, that not only reminds us of the meaning of our consecration but actually expresses the gift of ourselves to Jesus through Mary.

While several of the saints we've learned from during these past weeks have written excellent prayers or "formulas" of consecration, I'm not going to present their formulas here. (If you're interested, I've included them in Appendix One.) Instead, I'm going to present an updated prayer of consecration that combines the main insights we've covered during the retreat. Even though I'm no saint, I feel confident to do this because I'm making use of the actual words and ideas of all four of the Marian saints of our retreat. Moreover, I feel emboldened to compose this new prayer because of the words of Pope Pius XII on the occasion of St. Louis de Montfort's canonization:

True devotion ... aims essentially at union with Jesus under the guidance of Mary. *The form and practice of this devotion may vary according to time, place, and personal inclination.* Within the bounds of sound and safe doctrine, of orthodoxy and dignity of worship, *the Church leaves her children a just margin of liberty.* She is conscious that true and perfect devotion to Our Lady *is not bound up in any particular modes* in such a way that one of them can claim a monopoly over the others.[118]

Inspired by these words and taking the liberty the Pope gives us, I offer the following updated prayer of consecration that aims to capture the essentials of what we've learned during our retreat. Now, if it doesn't fit with your personal inclination, don't worry. You can always take the liberty to write your own prayer or use one written by the saints. Anyway, here's a summary statement of what we've learned, a statement that's also a prayer from the heart:

I, _____, a repentant sinner, renew and ratify today in your hands, O Immaculate Mother, the vows of my Baptism. I renounce Satan and resolve to follow Jesus Christ even more closely than before.

Mary, I give you my heart. Please set it on fire with love for Jesus. Make it always attentive to his burning thirst for love and for souls. Keep my heart in your most pure Heart that I may love Jesus and the members of his Body with your own perfect love.

Mary, I entrust myself totally to you: my body and soul, my goods, both interior and exterior, and even the value of all my good actions. Please make of me, of all that I am and have, whatever most pleases you. Let me be a fit instrument in your immaculate and merciful hands for bringing the greatest possible glory to God. If I fall, please lead me back to Jesus. Wash me in the blood and water that flow from his pierced side, and help me never to lose my trust in this fountain of love and mercy.

With you, O Immaculate Mother — you who always do the will of God — I unite myself to the perfect consecration of Jesus as he offers himself in the Spirit to the Father for the life of the world. Amen.

Tomorrow, you'll consecrate yourself (or re-consecrate yourself) totally to Jesus through Mary. And that's great! To do this, though, you'll need a prayer of consecration. Whether you use the one I just presented, one from the saints, or one of your own making, I encourage you to meditate on its meaning today. Such meditation on the prayer of consecration is a perfect preparation for Consecration Day.

By the way, you might want to read ahead to the first section of tomorrow's reading, entitled "Before the Consecration."

DAY OF CONSECRATION
A Glorious New Morning

Before Consecration

Congratulations! You've made it to Consecration Day. Now get ready for a gloriously new morning in your spiritual life. Of course, you're already ready. You've been faithfully preparing for this moment for the last 33 days. So here are just three things I recommend by way of final preparation: (1) Make a good confession — but if you don't have time to do so before the consecration, then from your heart tell the Lord you're sorry for your sins, and make a resolution to go to confession as soon as you reasonably can. (2) Write out or print up the prayer of consecration, so you can sign it after you've recited it. (3) Get a miraculous medal to wear around your neck as a sign of your consecration — or at least keep one in your purse or wallet. (See explanation of the miraculous medal in Appendix Two.) Again, these three things are recommendations. They're not essential to the consecration.

Prayer of Consecration

Okay, so you're ready to make your consecration. Now you'll need the right prayer. You can use either the one that follows, one from the saints, or one that you write yourself. Whatever prayer you use, I recommend that you recite it after attending Mass or even after receiving Holy Communion (if there's time). If you can't get to Mass, you can still make the consecration — Mass is highly recommended but not essential. With or without Mass, after you recite the consecration prayer, I suggest that you sign it, date it, and keep it in a safe place. (When I renew my consecration annually, I like to recite the prayer from the original copy and then sign and date it again.) Anyway, once again, here's the *33 Days to Morning Glory* Prayer of Consecration that summarizes the main ideas of our four Marian giants:

> I, _____, a repentant sinner, renew and ratify today in your hands, O Immaculate Mother, the vows of my Baptism. I renounce Satan and resolve to follow Jesus Christ even more closely than before.

Mary, I give you my heart. Please set it on fire with love for Jesus. Make it always attentive to his burning thirst for love and for souls. Keep my heart in your most pure Heart that I may love Jesus and the members of his Body with your own perfect love.

Mary, I entrust myself totally to you: my body and soul, my goods, both interior and exterior, and even the value of all my good actions. Please make of me, of all that I am and have, whatever most pleases you. Let me be a fit instrument in your immaculate and merciful hands for bringing the greatest possible glory to God. If I fall, please lead me back to Jesus. Wash me in the blood and water that flow from his pierced side, and help me never to lose my trust in this fountain of love and mercy.

With you, O Immaculate Mother — you who always do the will of God — I unite myself to the perfect consecration of Jesus as he offers himself in the Spirit to the Father for the life of the world. Amen.

After Consecration

What comes after we make our Marian consecration? Lots of grace and a gloriously new morning! But as morning turns into day, we may begin to wonder how we should live out our consecration. Do we just make it once and then forget about it? No. The following three points will help us live it out to the full: renewal, attitude, and devotion.

RENEWAL

Saint Louis de Montfort recommends that we renew our consecration at least once a year on the same day, though he would encourage us to renew it even more frequently. Pope John Paul renewed his consecration to Mary *every day*. For daily renewal, we can use the same full formula that we recite on Consecration Day or we can pray a shorter version such as this one:

> Mary, my Mother, I give myself totally to you as your
> possession and property. Please make of me, of all that
> I am and have, whatever most pleases you. Let me be
> a fit instrument in your immaculate and merciful
> hands for bringing the greatest possible glory to God.

Another way to renew and even deepen our Marian consecration is by making this retreat, *33 Days to Morning Glory*, with a group (or groups) from your parish. The group retreat, which includes a retreat companion and accompanying DVD, is a great way to enrich our understanding of Marian consecration. The group retreat also happens to be the first stage of an evangelization and faith-formation initiative called Hearts Afire: Parish-based Programs from the Marian Fathers of the Immaculate Conception. To learn more about this group retreat, see the information pages at the end of this book.

ATTITUDE

How should we live out our consecration? What kind of "Marian attitude" should we have? This is difficult to explain fully, and it will vary from person to person. Even our four saints differ in the way they express it. Still, they share the essentials.

Saint Louis de Montfort says that it's not enough to give ourselves to Mary just once and then be on our way. He believes we need to enter into the spirit of consecration, which requires an interior dependence on Mary. In other words, he explains that we should do everything "with Mary, in Mary, through Mary, and for Mary"[119] so as to do it all the more perfectly with Jesus, in Jesus, through Jesus, and for Jesus. De Montfort homes in especially on the "with Mary" idea and describes it using language that St. Maximilian Kolbe will later adopt:

> The essential practice of this devotion is to perform
> all our actions with Mary. ... We must have habitual
> recourse to our Lady, becoming one with her and
> adopting her intentions ... . In other words, we must

become an instrument in Mary's hands for her to act in us and do with us what she pleases, for the greater glory of her Son; and through Jesus for the greater glory of the Father. In this way, we pursue our interior life and make spiritual progress only in dependence on Mary.[120]

While Kolbe describes his consecration to Mary in a way similar to this citation ("instrument in Mary's hands"), he believes that "no fixed formula exists" for living the consecration.[121] He thinks that Mary herself needs to teach us what it means: "I don't know anything, either in theory and still less in practice, about how one can serve the Immaculata … . She alone must instruct each one of us at every moment, [and] lead us … ."[122] To receive Mary's instructions, we need to turn to her "through humble prayer" and reflect on "the loving experience" of her intercession in our daily lives.[123] In sum, for Kolbe, we learn the attitude of consecration *by relying on Mary's powerful intercession, experiencing her tender care, speaking to her from our hearts, letting ourselves be led by her, having recourse to her in all things, and trusting her completely.* Also, Kolbe would say that our consecration to Mary should give us an apostolic spirit that seeks to inspire others to make the consecration. For, as we learned earlier, Marian consecration is not just the quickest, easiest, and surest way to holiness for you and for me but *for everyone,* and thus, it's the most efficient way to bring the whole world to God in Christ.

For Blessed Mother Teresa, the living out of Marian consecration is essentially an attitude of the heart. More specifically, it's a living with and in Mary's Immaculate Heart. This attitude is described in detail in her "consecration covenant," which we read earlier. Moreover, the context for her entire consecration is found in a kind of compassion on Jesus who thirsts for love and for souls. So, for Mother Teresa, the attitude of living the consecration is one of allowing Mary to bring us to the Cross of Jesus, of letting her quiet us so we can hear Jesus' painful thirst, and of asking her to teach us to console Jesus with her own pure love.

Pope John Paul II finds the core of how we should live out our entrustment to Mary in words from the Gospel of John, "And from that hour the disciple took her to his own home" (Jn 19:27). In other words, he understands the attitude of entrustment as bringing Mary into everything that makes up one's inner life. As the "Pope of Suffering," he also gives a "co-redemptive" emphasis to his theology of Marian entrustment. He does this when he points out that she who was most fully united to Christ in his redemptive consecration of himself on the Cross helps us to unite ourselves to this same consecration. In other words, Mary helps us to "offer up" our own crosses; she reminds us not to waste our suffering; and she gives us the courage to be "co-redeemers" with Christ (see Col 1:24) — of course, in a way that is subordinate and united to Christ.[124]

What we see in all these saints and blesseds, however they express it, is that we should draw close to Mary, lovingly depend on her, speak to her from our hearts, have confidence in her powerful intercession, and share with her our joys, sorrows, and sufferings. Having said this, being consecrated to Mary is not based on feelings or even a constant mindfulness of Mary, as beautiful as such mindfulness is. According to St. Maximilian Kolbe, the proper attitude of those who are consecrated to Mary flows not so much from reason or emotions but from the will:

> [I]t is not at all necessary that the thought of the Immaculata should occur to [one's] mind ... for the essence of our union with her does not consist in thought, memory, or sentiment, but in our will.[125]

> I continue to say: we belong to her even if we do not constantly repeat this concrete offering [of a particular action to her], because we consecrated ourselves to her once, and we have never taken back our consecration.[126]

> [E]ven when we are not thinking of it ... [Mary] directs every one of our actions, prearranges all the circumstances, repairs the damage of our falls and

leads us lovingly toward heaven, and through us she is pleased to implant good ideas, sentiments, and examples everywhere in order to save souls and lead them to the good Jesus.[127]

So, while St. Louis de Montfort says, "We must never go to our Lord except through Mary,"[128] Kolbe teaches us that this going through her does not always have to be a conscious act. He would surely say that it's a good thing to explicitly turn to Mary, but it's not necessary to do this every time we turn to Jesus. He believes that once we've consecrated ourselves to Mary and develop an habitual dependence on her, we always do go to Jesus with her, even if we're not thinking of it. It's like this: Let's say a husband loves his wife and has to leave for a business trip, far from home. While he's travelling, meeting with clients, and filling out reports, his wife is still with him, in his heart, even if he's not explicitly thinking of her. So it is with us when Mary is in our hearts.

When we're fully consecrated to Mary, when we've developed a relationship of childlike dependence on her motherly care, she's always with us whenever we pray, just as Jesus is always with us whenever we pray to the Father. This latter point is true, for example, even if we don't explicitly turn to Jesus when we say, "Our Father." Kolbe's main idea here is that the Father, the Son, and Mary, who is always united with the Holy Spirit (while remaining a creature), do not live along parallel lines. Rather, Jesus, Mary, and the Holy Spirit are always united together in one movement "upward" to the Father, and whenever we turn to one of them, we join all of them in their one upward movement. In other words, they're not in competition; they don't take away from each other. Rather, they form a unity and work as a team — though with different roles — to bring all back to the Father.

I'd like to emphasize one important point before we conclude: While it's true that the effects of Marian consecration hold even when we're not thinking about Mary, living the consecration does require some effort. After all, deep relationships require communication and work, and this definitely applies to our relationship with Mary. The "communication" part refers to developing a loving dependence on her and turning to her in prayer, which we've already learned about in this section and about which we'll learn even more in the next. The "work" part refers to avoiding sin, which breaks both Jesus' and Mary's Hearts. Let me be clear: To be fully consecrated to Mary does *not* mean we won't still sin. However, it does mean that we should have a sincere resolution to avoid at least all mortal sin and that we should truly strive to grow in virtue and holiness. This is such a crucial part of Marian consecration that, as you'll recall, de Montfort begins his prayer of consecration with a renewal of our baptismal promises to reject Satan (sin) and follow Jesus Christ more closely.

In conclusion, if we're fully consecrated to Mary, then she works in our lives, augments our good works, and cares for us and our loved ones even when we don't have recourse to her. Moreover, with the Holy Spirit, she leads us to Jesus regardless of whether or not we're thinking of her. Such is the power of her motherhood. Such is the power of Marian consecration! Because of the greatness of this gift, we should strive all the more to unite ourselves with Mary and aim to do everything through her, with her, and in her. At least out of gratitude, we should make it our aim to have an attitude of growing mindfulness of and dependence on her. Yet there should be more at work here than just trying to be grateful to Mary. For the more we belong to her, the more she can use us to accomplish God's most perfect will. Indeed, the more we unite ourselves to Mary the more she can bring us into the deepest possible intimacy with Jesus. This is a mystery that she herself will teach us, a lesson we'll learn more from the experience of her loving care than from studying it in books.

DEVOTION

To help us deepen our attitude of loving dependence on Mary, it's a good idea to practice Marian devotions, especially those that are most connected to Marian consecration. Preeminent among these is the Rosary.

The Rosary fosters in us the attitude that I just described in the previous section. When we pray the Rosary, our focus should be on the mysteries of the life of Jesus. Yet the "Hail Marys," which faithfully flow in the background, foster in us the habitual attitude of being with Mary even as we're going to Jesus. In other words, even if we aren't thinking of the words of each Hail Mary, the words are still there, helping us to contemplate Christ. For a full treatment of the Rosary, see Appendix Two.

Other Marian devotions treated in Appendix Two are the scapular, miraculous medal, Chaplet of the 10 Evangelical Virtues, and the Chaplet of the Seven Sorrows. Marian devotions not treated in Appendix Two but that deserve mention and a brief description are novenas, icons, pilgrimages, feast days, confraternities, and spiritual reading.

NOVENAS. From the Latin word "*novem*," meaning nine, a novena is typically a nine-day period of prayer to obtain special graces or to implore particular petitions. Novenas tend to convey a sense of urgency. Prayed every day for nine days, the prayer can be as simple as a single Hail Mary or as elaborate as the Litany of Loreto. (See Appendix One for this prayer.) Sometimes, an intention is so urgent that we don't have nine days beforehand to pray. For instance, maybe you've just been granted a job interview, but it's scheduled for this afternoon! Well, you might try Blessed Mother Teresa's "flying novena," whereby one prays nine Memorare's in a row. (For the text of the Memorare prayer, see Appendix One.) Mother Teresa would often pray this novena whenever big problems or difficulties arose that needed an immediate dose of great grace. It's reported that she often experienced miraculous effects by praying it.

ICONS. Icons, or any tasteful images or representations of Jesus, Mary, the angels, or the saints, serve to turn our minds and hearts to God as they remind us of his presence and the loving intercession of Mary, the angels, and the saints. In 787, the Second Council of Nicea declared that holy images (including those of Mary) are to be used and venerated. When we venerate an image (be it a picture, statue, etc.), we're showing a sign of reverence toward the person whom the image represents. In our busy lives, placing pictures of Mary in our homes and even in our cars can remind us that she is always with us. We can also keep our favorite prayer cards in a pocket or purse. If you'd like to purchase a prayer card with the image from the cover of this book, please see the ad at the back.

*P*ILGRIMAGES. Pilgrimages lead us from the everyday rhythm and distractions of life to a graced place of prayer and encounter with the Lord. There are many Marian shrines and pilgrimage destinations around the U.S. and the world. For an exhaustive list, download our free Mary App for smartphones. (See ad at the end of this book.) Here are several North American Marian Shrines:

> Shrine of Ste. Anne de Beaupre
> 10018 Avenue Royale
> Ste-Anne-De-Beaupré, QC G0A 3C0 Canada
> 418-827-3781, ext. 2700
> www.ssadb.qc.ca/en/index.htm

> National Shrine of The Divine Mercy
> Marian Fathers of the Immaculate Conception
> Eden Hill
> Stockbridge, MA 01262
> 413-298-3931 (general questions)
> 413-298-1118 (pilgrimages)
> www.thedivinemercy.org/shrine

> Shrine of Our Lady of Martyrs
> 136 Shrine Road
> Fultonville, NY 12016
> 518-853-3033
> www.martyrshrine.org

> Basilica of the National Shrine
> of the Immaculate Conception
> 400 Michigan Avenue, Northeast
> Washington, D.C. 20017

202-526-8300
www.nationalshrine.com

Our Lady of the Angels Monastery
3222 County Road 548
Hanceville, AL 35077
256-352-6267 (general info)
205-795-5717 (group tours)
www.olamshrine.com

Basilica of Our Lady of Guadalupe
Plaza de las Américas,
Núm. 1, Col. Villa de Guadalupe. México D.F, C.P. 07050
Phone: 55 77 60 22
www.virgendeguadalupe.org.mx

*F*EAST *DAYS*. Those who are consecrated to Mary should celebrate her feast days with particular fervor and love. According to one of Pope Benedict XVI's favorite philosophers, Joseph Pieper, man's true lack "would be his inability to celebrate a feast in a truly festive fashion." He goes on:

> To [celebrate a feast] requires, as everybody knows, that the reality of our life and our world be first wholeheartedly accepted and that this acceptance, then, on special occasions, be expressed and lived out in exceptional ritual: this indeed is what it means to "celebrate a feast"![129]

For those of us who are consecrated to Jesus through Mary, a big part of the "reality of our life and our world" is our consecration, our belonging to God through the Mother of God. Therefore, because we "wholeheartedly accept" this, on "special occasions," such as Marian feasts, we should express our joy in belonging to Mary and live it out in an "exceptional" way. We should truly celebrate Mary's feasts as occasions to express our joy in belonging to God through her.

For a list of the Church's main Marian feast days and more information about Marian feasts, see the following endnote.[130]

For an explanation of the "First Saturday" devotion that was introduced by Our Lady of Fatima, refer to this endnote.[131] Speaking of Saturday, Saturday Masses are frequently offered in honor of the Blessed Virgin Mary.

CONFRATERNITIES. A confraternity is typically a voluntary association of the faithful joined by a common spirituality and cooperation in certain good works. Confraternities were established in the Middle Ages when many lay people wished to participate in some way in the spiritual life of religious orders. The Confraternity of the Immaculate Conception of the Most Blessed Virgin Mary that exists with the Congregation of Marian Fathers of the Immaculate Conception promotes devotion to the Immaculate Conception of Mary, so her motherly love might strengthen, comfort, and fill hearts with joy, the source of which is her Son, Jesus Christ, our Savior. The external sign of belonging to the Confraternity is the blue scapular. (See Appendix Two to learn about the scapular devotion and how to join the Confraternity of the Blue Scapular.)

SPIRITUAL READING. Saint Theresa of Avila once wrote that for 18 years she would never go to pray without a spiritual book.[132] Spiritual reading can be of great benefit to our life of prayer and help us to deepen our relationship with Mary; for it's often the case that the more we know someone the better we're able to love them. Prayerfully reading good Marian books can be a great way to get to know Mary. In fact, we might want to get into the practice, as some saints did, of reading Marian books at least on Saturdays. (Saturdays are traditionally dedicated to Mary.) Here are some books on Mary (or Marian saints) that I recommend:

Apostoli, Fr. Andrew, CFR, *Fatima For Today: The Urgent Marian Message of Hope* (San Francisco: Ignatius Press, 2010).

De Montfort, St. Louis, *True Devotion to Mary.*

Frossard, André, *Forget Not Love: The Passion of St. Maximilian Kolbe* (San Francisco: Ignatius Press, 1991).

Hahn, Scott, *Hail, Holy Queen: The Mother of God in the Word of God* (NY: Doubleday, 2001).

John Paul II, Pope, *Encyclical Letter: Redemptoris Mater* (Mother of the Redeemer, 1987).

John Paul II, Pope, *Apostolic Letter: Rosarium Virginis Mariae* (Rosary of the Blessed Virgin Mary, 2002).

Langford, MC, Joseph, *Mother Teresa: In the Shadow of Our Lady: Sharing Mother Teresa's Mystical Relationship with Mary* (Huntington, IN: Our Sunday Visitor, 2007).

Laurentin, René, *Bernadette Speaks: A Life of Saint Bernadette Soubirous in Her Own Words* (Boston: Pauline Books and Media, 2000).

Miravalle, Mark, *Know Your Mother: A Complete Introduction to Mary* (Stockbridge, MA: Marian Press, 2014).

Miravalle, Mark, *Meet Your Mother: A Brief Introduction to Mary* (Stockbridge, MA: Marian Press, 2014).

Prayers

Consecration Prayers

Morning Glory Consecration Prayer

I, _____, a repentant sinner, renew and ratify today in your hands, O Immaculate Mother, the vows of my Baptism. I renounce Satan and resolve to follow Jesus Christ even more closely than before.

Mary, I give you my heart. Please set it on fire with love for Jesus. Make it always attentive to his burning thirst for love and for souls. Keep my heart in your most pure Heart that I may love Jesus and the members of his Body with your own perfect love.

Mary, I entrust myself totally to you: my body and soul, my goods, both interior and exterior, and even the value of all my good actions. Please make of me, of all that I am and have, whatever most pleases you. Let me be a fit instrument in your immaculate and merciful hands for bringing the greatest possible glory to God. If I fall, please lead me back to Jesus. Wash me in the blood and water that flow from his pierced side, and help me never to lose my trust in this fountain of love and mercy.

With you, O Immaculate Mother — you who always do the will of God — I unite myself to the perfect consecration of Jesus as he offers himself in the Spirit to the Father for the life of the world. Amen.

Morning Glory Consecration Prayer
(Short Version)

Mary, my Mother, I give myself totally to you as your possession and property. Please make of me, of all that I am and have, whatever most pleases you. Let me be a fit instrument in your immaculate and merciful hands for bringing the greatest possible glory to God. Amen.

Consecration Prayer of St. Louis de Montfort

I, _____, a faithless sinner, renew and ratify today in thy hands the vows of my Baptism; I renounce forever Satan, his pomps and works; and I give myself entirely to Jesus Christ, the Incarnate Wisdom, to carry my cross after Him all the days of my life, and to be more faithful to Him than I have ever been before. In the presence of all the heavenly court I choose thee this day for my Mother and Mistress. I deliver and consecrate to thee, as thy slave, my body and soul, my goods, both interior and exterior, and even the value of all my good actions, past, present, and future; leaving to thee the entire and full right of disposing of me, and all that belongs to me, without exception, according to thy good pleasure, for the greater glory of God in time and in eternity. Amen.

Consecration Prayer of St. Maximilian Kolbe

O Immaculata, Queen of Heaven and earth, refuge of sinners and our most loving Mother, God has willed to entrust the entire order of mercy to you. I, _____, a repentant sinner, cast myself at your feet humbly imploring you to take me with all that I am and have, wholly to yourself as your possession and property. Please make of me, of all my powers of soul and body, of my whole life, death, and eternity, whatever most pleases you. If it pleases you, use all that I am and have without reserve, wholly to accomplish what was said of you: "She will crush your head," and, "You alone have destroyed all heresies in the whole world."

Let me be a fit instrument in your immaculate and merciful hands for introducing and increasing your glory to the maximum in all the many strayed and indifferent souls, and thus help extend as far as possible the blessed kingdom of the most Sacred Heart of Jesus. For wherever you enter you obtain the grace of conversion and growth in holiness, since it is through your hands that all graces come to us from the most Sacred Heart of Jesus.

V. Allow me to praise you, O Sacred Virgin.
R. Give me strength against your enemies.

Consoler Consecration to Mary

Today I renew my total consecration to you, Mary, my mother. I give you my whole being so you may lead me to console your Son with the perfect consolation you give to him. From this day forward, dear Jesus, whenever I embrace you, may it be with the arms of Mary. Whenever I kiss you, may it be with the lips of Mary. Whenever I sing to you, praise you, and thank you, may it be with the voice of Mary. Jesus, in short, every time I love you, may it be with the Heart of Mary. Amen.

Consoler Consecration to Mary
(Short Version)

Mary, I want to be a saint. I know that you also want me to be a saint and that it's your God-given mission to form me into one. So, Mary, at this moment, on this day, I freely choose to give you my full permission to do your work in me, with your Spouse, the Holy Spirit. Amen.

Other Marian Prayers

Hail Mary

Hail, Mary, full of grace; the Lord is with thee; blessed art thou among women, and blessed is the fruit of thy womb, Jesus. Holy Mary, Mother of God, pray for us sinners, now and at the hour of our death. Amen.

Sub Tuum Praesidium
("Under Your Patronage" — c. 250 AD)

We fly to your patronage,
O Holy Mother of God,
Despise not our petitions in our necessities,
But deliver us from all danger,
O ever glorious and blessed Virgin. Amen.

The Memorare

Remember, O most gracious Virgin Mary, that never was it known, that anyone who fled to thy protection, implored thy help, or sought thy intercession, was left unaided. Inspired by this confidence, I fly unto thee, O Virgin of virgins, my Mother. To thee do I come, before thee I stand, sinful and sorrowful. O Mother of the Word Incarnate, despise not my petitions, but in thy mercy hear and answer me. Amen.

Hail, Holy Queen

Hail, Holy Queen, Mother of Mercy, our life, our sweetness, and our hope. To thee do we cry, poor banished children of Eve; to thee do we send up our sighs, mourning and weeping in this valley of tears. Turn then, most gracious advocate, thine eyes of mercy toward us; and after this our exile show unto us the blessed fruit of thy womb, Jesus. O clement, O loving, O sweet Virgin Mary.

V. Pray for us, O holy Mother of God.
R. That we may be made worthy of the promises of Christ.

The Angelus
(Traditionally prayed at morning, noon, and evening)

V. The angel of the Lord declared unto Mary,
R. And she conceived by the Holy Spirit.
   Hail Mary…

V. Behold, the handmaid of the Lord,
R. Be it done to me according to Thy word.
   Hail Mary…

V. And the Word was made flesh,
R. And dwelt among us.
   Hail Mary…

V. Pray for us, O holy Mother of God.
R. That we may be made worthy of the promises of Christ.

Let us pray: Pour forth, we beseech Thee, O Lord, Thy grace into our hearts, that we, to whom the Incarnation of Christ, Thy Son, was made known by the message of an angel, may, by His Passion and Cross, be brought to the glory of His Resurrection, through the same Christ our Lord. Amen.

Regina Caeli
(Said during the Easter season in place of the Angelus)

O Queen of Heaven, rejoice, alleluia,
For He whom you did merit to bear, alleluia,
Has risen as He said, alleluia:
Pray for us to God, alleluia.

> V. Rejoice and be glad, O Virgin Mary, alleluia.
> R. Because the Lord has truly risen, alleluia.

Let us pray. O God, You were pleased to give joy to the world through the resurrection of Your Son, our Lord Jesus Christ; grant, we beseech You, that through His mother, the Virgin Mary, we may obtain the joys of everlasting life. Through the same Christ our Lord. Amen.

> V. Glory be to the Father, etc.

Alma Redemptoris

Loving mother of the Redeemer,
Gate of heaven, star of the sea,
Assist your people who have fallen yet strive to rise again.
To the wonderment of nature you bore your Creator,
Yet remained a virgin after as before.
You who received Gabriel's joyful greeting,
Have pity on us poor sinners.

Ave Maris Stella

Hail, bright star of ocean,
God's own Mother blest,
Ever sinless Virgin,
Gate of heavenly rest.

Taking that sweet Ave
Which from Gabriel came,
Peace confirm within us,
Changing Eva's name.

Break the captives' fetters,
Light on blindness pour,
All our ills expelling,
Every bliss implore.

Show thyself a Mother;
May the Word Divine,
Born for us thine Infant,
Hear our prayers through thine.

Virgin all excelling,
Mildest of the mild,
Freed from guilt, preserve us,
Pure and undefiled.

Keep our life all spotless,
Make our way secure,
Till we find in Jesus
Joy for evermore.

Through the highest heaven
To the immortal Three,
Father, Son, and Spirit,
One same glory be. Amen.

Litany of Loreto

Lord have mercy on us.
   Lord have mercy on us.
Christ have mercy on us.
   Christ have mercy on us.
Lord have mercy on us.
   Lord have mercy on us.
Christ, hear us.
   Christ, graciously hear us.

God the Father of Heaven, *have mercy on us.*
God the Son, Redeemer of the world, *have mercy on us.*
God the Holy Spirit, *have mercy on us.*
Holy Trinity, one God, *have mercy on us.*

Holy Mary, *pray for us.*
Holy Mother of God, *pray for us.*
Mother of the Church, *pray for us.*
Holy Virgin of virgins, *pray for us.*
Mother of Christ, *pray for us.*
Mother of divine grace, *pray for us.*
Mother most pure, *pray for us.*
Mother most chaste, *pray for us.*
Mother inviolate, *pray for us.*
Mother undefiled, *pray for us.*
Mother most amiable, *pray for us.*
Mother most admirable, *pray for us.*
Mother of good counsel, *pray for us.*
Mother of our Creator, *pray for us.*
Mother of our Redeemer, *pray for us.*
Virgin most prudent, *pray for us.*
Virgin most venerable, *pray for us.*
Virgin most renowned, *pray for us.*
Virgin most powerful, *pray for us.*
Virgin most merciful, *pray for us.*
Virgin most faithful, *pray for us.*
Mirror of justice, *pray for us.*
Seat of wisdom, *pray for us.*
Cause of our joy, *pray for us.*
Spiritual vessel, *pray for us.*
Vessel of honor, *pray for us.*
Singular vessel of devotion, *pray for us.*
Mystical rose, *pray for us.*
Tower of David, *pray for us.*
Tower of ivory, *pray for us.*
House of gold, *pray for us.*
Ark of the covenant, *pray for us.*

Gate of Heaven, *pray for us.*
Morning Star, *pray for us.*
Health of the sick, *pray for us.*
Refuge of sinners, *pray for us.*
Comforter of the afflicted, *pray for us.*
Help of Christians, *pray for us.*
Queen of Angels, *pray for us.*
Queen of Patriarchs, *pray for us.*
Queen of Prophets, *pray for us.*
Queen of Apostles, *pray for us.*
Queen of Martyrs, *pray for us.*
Queen of Confessors, *pray for us.*
Queen of Virgins, *pray for us.*
Queen of all Saints, *pray for us.*
Queen conceived without original sin, *pray for us.*
Queen of the most holy Rosary, *pray for us.*
Queen of the family, *pray for us.*
Queen of peace, *pray for us.*

Lamb of God, Who takes away the sins of the world:
    Spare us, O Lord.
Lamb of God, Who takes away the sins of the world:
    Graciously hear us, O Lord.
Lamb of God, Who takes away the sins of the world:
    Have mercy on us.

Pray for us, O holy Mother of God,
    That we may be made worthy of the promises of Christ.

Let us pray.

Grant, we beseech you, O Lord God, that we your servants, may enjoy lasting health of mind and body, and by the glorious intercession of the Blessed Mary, ever Virgin, be delivered from present sorrow and enter into the joy of eternal happiness. Through Christ our Lord.

R. Amen.

Fatima Prayers

My God, I believe, I adore, I hope, and I love you! I beg pardon of you for those who do not believe, do not adore, do not hope, and do not love you.

Most Holy Trinity, Father, Son, and Holy Spirit, I adore you profoundly and offer you the most precious Body, Blood, Soul and Divinity of Jesus Christ present in all the tabernacles of the world, in reparation for the outrages, sacrileges, and indifferences with which he is offended. And through the infinite merits of his most Sacred Heart and the Immaculate Heart of Mary, I beg of you the conversion of poor sinners.

APPENDIX TWO
Devotions

The Rosary

Introduction

In this section on the Rosary, I want to do three things: (1) teach what the Rosary is, (2) explain why we should pray it, and (3) give instructions on how to pray it.

What is the Rosary?

The Rosary is a tool that helps us to pray. It's made up of a string of about 60 beads, each of which represents a particular prayer to be said. Most of the beads are reserved for the Hail Mary prayer. Others are for the Our Father, Glory be, etc. But the Rosary is much more than the sum of these prayers. In fact, it leads us into deep meditation and contemplation of the face of Christ. Moreover, it helps us enter the school of Mary, who taught Jesus to pray and wants to teach us to pray as well. Ever wonder how to pray? The Rosary offers a complete way of prayer that includes the three forms of prayer: vocal prayer, meditation, and even contemplation.

The Rosary's completeness, simplicity, and depth flow from its structure. It consists of 20 sets of 10 Hail Marys — often called "decades" — punctuated by Our Fathers, Glory Bes, and the "O My Jesus" Fatima prayer. Each of the 20 sets of 10 Hail Marys is dedicated to a particular event or "mystery" from Sacred Scripture, which is to be meditated and contemplated while the prayers are said. For example, while one is reciting the 10 Hail Marys, he can reflect on and ponder in his heart the Birth of Jesus.

The 20 events or mysteries of the Rosary are divided into four categories: The Joyful, Luminous, Sorrowful, and Glorious Mysteries that, together, provide a complete summary of the life of Jesus. Now, it might seem daunting to meditate on the entire life of Jesus all at once. This is why most people who pray the Rosary every day don't meditate on all 20 mysteries in one day. Instead, they break it up by daily praying a fourth of the full Rosary (one of the four categories of mysteries). This seems to be encouraged by a tradition in the Church that dedicates certain days of the week to praying one of the four sets of mysteries of the Rosary:

- Monday and Saturday: Joyful
- Tuesday and Friday: Sorrowful
- Wednesday and Sunday: Glorious
- Thursday: Luminous

You'll notice that the Luminous Mysteries only get one day of the week while the other mysteries get two. This may be because the Luminous Mysteries are the newcomers, added relatively recently (2002) by Pope John Paul II. In his beautiful apostolic letter on the Rosary, *Rosarium Virginis Mariae*, the Pope explains why he added them. (This letter can easily be found online.[133])

John Paul's addition of the Luminous Mysteries was the first major change to the Rosary since the Church approved its present form in 1569. Prior to 1569, the Rosary had gone through a period of development following the original inspiration that was given to St. Dominic in the 13th century, reportedly by the Blessed Mother herself.

Why Pray the Rosary?

A woman was once asked why she prayed the Rosary every day. She looked away for a moment, looked back at her questioner, and replied, "All I can tell you is if I say a Rosary, the day works; and if I don't, nothing works." This is true. It's not true because of some kind of magic or superstition. It's true because of Mary's maternal intercession and the power of the mysteries of the life of Christ.

I could spend a lot of time here describing how Pope after Pope has encouraged everyone to pray the Rosary, how they've called it one of the most powerful prayers there is after the liturgy, and how they've granted a ton of indulgences to those who pray it. I could also tell story after story of how this saint or that one was totally dedicated to praying the Rosary and received miracle upon miracle through praying it. Instead of going into all of this, though, I'd like to dwell on just three points: Mary, the battle of prayer, and the significance of the Mysteries.

*M*ARY. During the last two centuries, people have witnessed more Church-approved Marian apparitions than during all other centuries combined. Why such an increase? Because of the difficulties of modern times. Mary has been coming to earth and appearing to people in our day to give warnings about bad things that will happen if people don't repent and pray the Rosary.

Our Blessed Mother loves her children and doesn't want us to suffer calamities, so she encourages us to pray the Rosary. She wants us to experience peace in our families, societies, and nations, so she asks us to pray the Rosary. She desires that sinners be converted and people experience the abundant life in Christ, so she tells us to pray the Rosary. Mary has made it very clear, through the testimony of Church-approved apparitions, that she wants us to pray the Rosary. In fact, sometimes, even with tears in her eyes, she pleads with us to pray it. This should be enough for us — yet there's more. The Rosary isn't just an instrument for world peace.

Praying the Rosary is a place to meet Mary. It's one of the best ways to develop the loving attitude of dependence on her that we learned about during our reading for Consecration Day. There's something about praying the Rosary that helps us develop a filial attitude of being with Mary. I think this has to do with the peaceful rhythm of the Hail Marys. When we pray the Rosary, the goal is not so much to reflect on the words of the Hail Mary prayer itself. Rather, the Hail Marys are meant to be a kind of "background music" that helps us enter into contemplation of the mysteries. This background music is like the gentle hand of a mother on our shoulders, standing behind us, getting us to look at Jesus, contemplate his face, and love him through his mother's eyes, mind, and heart. Praying the Rosary does something to the soul. It allows Mary to shape and form us according to the image of her Son. Pope John Paul II puts it like this:

> The Rosary mystically transports us to Mary's side as she is busy watching over the human growth of Christ

in the home of Nazareth. This enables her to train us
and to mold us with the same care.[134]

To be formed and molded into Christ with the same loving
care that Christ himself received from Mary! This is what Marian
consecration is all about, and it's why we should pray the Rosary.
But how does Mary form and mold us? By the mysteries of the
life of her Son and by the lesson of her own humble, loving, and
docile attitude before the majesty of God. Pondering and living
the mysteries of the Rosary are keys to holiness.

*T*HE BATTLE OF PRAYER. Unfortunately, we may not always
fully enter into the mysteries of Christ, because we don't
persevere in praying the Rosary. We forget that, as the *Catechism
of the Catholic Church* teaches, prayer can be a real battle.[135]
Sometimes the attacks in this battle are dryness in praying the
Rosary. Well, we should keep praying it. Sometimes, as we get
ready to pray the Rosary, we suddenly feel an aversion, fatigue
comes over us, and our minds think of a million other things
that have to be done. We should keep praying it. Sometimes, it's
true, we do have pressing duties that are more important to
attend to than praying the Rosary. But sometimes the things we
"have" to do can be a temptation and poor excuse not to pray
the Rosary. For instance, how much time do we waste on needless
e-mail, social networking websites, television, and phone calls?
Can't we cut out just 20 minutes from such time-wasting activity
to pray the Rosary? Why is it so hard sometimes to break away
and pray? Again, it's because prayer is a battle. Satan doesn't
want us to enter into the power of the mysteries of the life of
Christ. He wants us to stay complacent, lukewarm, and lazy. He
wants us to be satisfied with mediocrity.

The mysteries of the life of Christ are powerful, and we can
receive their power through praying the Rosary — but for this
to happen, we need to pray it *well*. Here's what I'm getting at:
The battle of prayer does not always end when we make the Sign
of the Cross and begin to pray the Rosary. The battle can
continue, and too often when we pray the Rosary, we don't keep
up the fight. We give in to distractions. We don't ponder the

mysteries. We let our minds wander. Of course, distractions in prayer are common. But are we vigilant in at least trying to stay focused? Or are we just thinking about getting the Rosary over with so we can get back to "the more important things." No, the Rosary is incredibly important, and we should strive to pray it even better. One way to help us pray it better is by reading John Paul's letter on the Rosary, which I mentioned earlier. Reading it will help renew our fervor for this grace-filled form of prayer. But before you go find his letter online, I'd like to end this section by saying a bit more about the mysteries of the life of Jesus, which are the heart of the Rosary.

THE SIGNIFICANCE OF THE MYSTERIES. The mysteries of the life of Jesus are packed with meaning. And they're so packed because Jesus is so unique. Of course, he's *not* unique in that he is like us in all things (except sin) — in other words, he's true man. But he *is* unique in that he's true God. He's the God-man. This is something that should always be at the back of our minds when we meditate on the mysteries of Jesus. This infant in Bethlehem, this child in Jerusalem, this man in Galilee — he's God. Why is he being born? Why is he in the Temple? What is he trying to teach us? We should ask ourselves these questions when we pray the Rosary. Now, because Jesus is God, everything he says and does is packed with meaning. In fact, the events of his life are so packed with meaning that we can't exhaust them. This is why we call the events "mysteries." A mystery doesn't mean we can't understand it. It means we can never come to the limit of understanding it. There are always more wonders to discover. There are always more riches to mine! There are infinite, inexhaustible treasures contained in each one of the mysteries of the life of Christ.

Something else about the mysteries: They're unique events. Again, they're unique because Jesus is so unique. He's God. And this is a big deal. In what is perhaps my favorite passage in the entire *Catechism of the Catholic Church*, the Church explains what's so unique about the events of the life of Jesus, and why they're such a big deal. It does so in explaining the Paschal mystery of Jesus (his suffering, death, and Resurrection), but what follows applies to all the events of his life:

His Paschal mystery is a real event that occurred in
our history, but it is unique: all other historical
events happen once, and then they pass away,
swallowed up in the past. The Paschal mystery of
Christ, by contrast, cannot remain only in the past,
because by his death he destroyed death, and all that
Christ is — all that he did and suffered for all men
— participates in the divine eternity, and so
transcends all times while being made present in
them all. The event of the Cross and Resurrection
abides and draws everything toward life.[136]

This mind-blowing passage captures an amazing point
about the mystery of time and eternity. When God, who lives in
eternity, steps into time as the Incarnate Word, this event, one
might say, "bends time," because it creates a unique historical
reality that mysteriously exists both inside and outside of time.
As the *Catechism* teaches, the mysteries of the life of Jesus *are
not swallowed up in the past*; rather, they are still here, now,
living — for us. "Jesus Christ is the same yesterday, today, and
tomorrow" (Heb 13:8). These events in our Savior's life share
in the "divine eternity," the "eternal now" of God. They are
truly present in *all times*, abiding forever. This reality deserves deep
meditation, and each mystery of the Rosary is an opportunity for
such meditation and for becoming fully present to Christ. By
way of example, let's take one mystery of the Rosary to see
what's going on here. Let's reflect on the fifth Sorrowful
Mystery, The Crucifixion.

About 2,000 years ago, Jesus was on the Cross, dying in
agony for our sins. As this was happening, Mary, St. John, and
St. Mary Magdalene were all historically present to Jesus on the
Cross. This means that they were literally, physically there, and
they could see, smell, hear, and feel what was going on around
them. Roman soldiers were also historically present there along
with Jewish priests and elders. Now, because the events of the
life of Jesus *abide* and are present in all times, *we also can be there*.
Of course, we can't be historically present there — we can't go

back in a time machine and be there physically — but we can still be truly present to Jesus dying on the Cross. In fact, we can be even more present to him than the Roman soldiers and Jewish priests and elders. How? By the virtues of faith and love. In other words, when our hearts are moved to *faith* and *love* as we ponder Jesus' suffering and death on the Cross, we are truly, "mystically transported" to him. We have a real contact with him there. We can truly receive, here and now, the fountain of love and mercy that gushes forth from Jesus' pierced side and that flows through the ages like a mighty river. Indeed, by the theological virtues of faith and love, we can enter into the "divine eternity" and become truly present to Jesus in all the mysteries of his life, death, and Resurrection — more so than if we had gone back in a time machine.

We enter into a real contact with Jesus through faith-filled and loving prayer even if, through meditation, we don't get all the historical details right. Who knows exactly how many people were historically present at the foot of the Cross or exactly what it all looked like? Historical details are not what are most important. The important thing is that we ponder the Scripture-based mystery in our hearts and that we do so with faith and love. Whenever the theological virtues (faith, hope, and love) are active when we pray, then we have a real contact with Jesus. We touch him by these virtues, and just as a divine, healing, and strengthening power went forth from Christ to all those who encountered him in faith during his earthly life (see Lk 6:19), so also today, when we meditate on the mysteries of the life of Christ in faith, hope, and love, that same divine power reaches us.

The power that goes forth from Christ to us in his mysteries is new, fresh, and unique in each mystery. For instance, the birth of Jesus contains it's own riches and power that can lift us up and enlighten our minds, giving us strength to be compassionate to the poor and to embrace at least spiritual poverty as we reflect on how Jesus is born in poverty. The graces are endless in each mystery, and their treasures are released when we ponder the mysteries, with Mary, in faith, hope, and love.

How to Pray the Rosary

1. Make the Sign of the Cross and pray the "Apostles' Creed." (All Rosary Prayers, such as the Apostles Creed, can be found in the next section.)

2. Pray the "Our Father."

3. Pray three "Hail Marys."

4. Pray the "Glory be to the Father."

5. Announce the First Mystery; then Pray the "Our Father."

6. Pray 10 "Hail Marys" while meditating on the Mystery.

7. Pray the "Glory be to the Father" followed by the prayer requested by Our Lady of Fatima: "O my Jesus, forgive us our sins, save us from the fires of hell, lead all souls to Heaven, especially those in most need of Thy mercy."

8. Announce the Second Mystery. Then pray the "Our Father." Repeat 6 and 7 and continue with the Third, Fourth, and Fifth Mysteries in the same manner.

9. Pray the "Hail, Holy Queen" on the medal after the five decades are completed.

10. Pray the optional closing prayer, if you wish, and then make the Sign of the Cross.

Rosary Prayers

The Sign of the Cross

In the name of the Father, and of the Son, and of the Holy Spirit. Amen.

The Apostles' Creed

I believe in God, the Father almighty, Creator of heaven and earth, and in Jesus Christ, his only Son, our Lord, who was conceived by the Holy Spirit, born of the Virgin Mary, suffered under Pontius Pilate, was crucified, died, and was buried; he descended into hell; on the third day he rose again from the dead; he ascended into heaven, and is seated at the right hand of God the Father almighty; from there he will come to judge the living and the dead. I believe in the Holy Spirit, the holy catholic Church, the communion of saints, the forgiveness of sins, the resurrection of the body, and life everlasting. Amen.

Our Father

Our Father, who art in heaven, hallowed be thy name; thy kingdom come; thy will be done on earth, as it is in heaven. Give us this day our daily bread; and forgive us our trespasses, as we forgive those who trespass against us; and lead us not into temptation, but deliver us from evil. Amen.

Hail Mary

Hail, Mary, full of grace; the Lord is with thee; blessed art thou among women, and blessed is the fruit of thy womb, Jesus. Holy Mary, Mother of God, pray for us sinners, now and at the hour of our death. Amen.

Glory Be

Glory be to the Father, and to the Son, and to the Holy Spirit. As it was in the beginning, is now, and ever shall be, world without end. Amen.

Fatima Prayer

O my Jesus, forgive us our sins, save us from the fires of hell. Lead all souls to Heaven, especially those in most need of thy mercy.

Hail, Holy Queen

Hail, Holy Queen, Mother of Mercy, our life, our sweetness, and our hope. To thee do we cry, poor banished children of Eve; to thee do we send up our sighs, mourning and weeping in this valley of tears. Turn then, most gracious advocate, thine eyes of mercy toward us; and after this our exile show unto us the blessed fruit of thy womb, Jesus. O clement, O loving, O sweet Virgin Mary.

> V. Pray for us, O holy Mother of God.
> R. That we may be made worthy of the promises of Christ.

Optional Closing Prayer

O God, whose only-begotten Son, by his life, death, and resurrection has purchased for us the rewards of eternal life; grant, we beseech thee, that, while meditating on these sacred mysteries of the most holy Rosary of the Blessed Virgin Mary, that we may imitate what they contain, and obtain what they promise. Through the same Christ our Lord. Amen.

Mysteries of the Rosary

The Joyful Mysteries

First Joyful Mystery:
THE ANNUNCIATION

And when the angel had come to her, he said, "Hail, full of grace, the Lord is with you" (Lk 1:28).

Our Father, 10 Hail Marys, Glory Be, etc.

FRUIT OF THE MYSTERY: *HUMILITY*

Second Joyful Mystery:
THE VISITATION

Elizabeth was filled with the Holy Spirit and cried out in a loud voice: "Blest are you among women and blest is the fruit of your womb" (Lk 1:41-42).

Our Father, 10 Hail Marys, Glory Be, etc.

FRUIT OF THE MYSTERY:
LOVE OF NEIGHBOR

Third Joyful Mystery:
THE BIRTH OF JESUS

She gave birth to her first-born Son and wrapped Him in swaddling clothes and laid Him in a manger, because there was no room for them in the place where travelers lodged (Lk 2:7).

Our Father, 10 Hail Marys, Glory Be, etc.
FRUIT OF THE MYSTERY: *POVERTY*

Fourth Joyful Mystery:
THE PRESENTATION

When the day came to purify them according to the law of Moses, the couple brought Him up to Jerusalem so that He could be presented to the Lord, for it is written in the law of the Lord, "Every first-born male shall be consecrated to the Lord" (Lk 2:22-23).

Our Father, 10 Hail Marys, Glory Be, etc.
FRUIT OF THE MYSTERY: *OBEDIENCE*

Fifth Joyful Mystery:
FINDING THE CHILD JESUS IN THE TEMPLE

On the third day they came upon Him in the temple sitting in the midst of the teachers, listening to them and asking them questions (Lk 2:46).

Our Father, 10 Hail Marys, Glory Be, etc.

FRUIT OF THE MYSTERY:
JOY IN FINDING JESUS

∿ The Luminous Mysteries ∿

First Luminous Mystery:
BAPTISM OF JESUS

And when Jesus was baptized, … the heavens were opened and He saw the Spirit of God descending like a dove, and alighting on Him, and lo, a voice from heaven, saying, "this is My beloved Son, with whom I am well pleased" (Mt 3:16-17).

Our Father, 10 Hail Marys, Glory Be, etc.

FRUIT OF THE MYSTERY:
OPENNESS TO THE HOLY SPIRIT

Second Luminous Mystery:
WEDDING AT CANA

His mother said to the servants, "Do whatever He tells you." Jesus said to them, "Fill the jars with water." And they filled them to the brim (Jn 2:5-7).

Our Father, 10 Hail Marys, Glory Be, etc.

FRUIT OF THE MYSTERY:
TO JESUS THROUGH MARY

Third Luminous Mystery:
PROCLAIMING THE KINGDOM

"And preach as you go, saying, 'The kingdom of heaven is at hand.' Heal the sick, raise the dead, cleanse lepers, cast out demons. You received without pay, give without pay" (Mt 10:7-8).

Our Father, 10 Hail Marys, Glory Be, etc.

FRUIT OF THE MYSTERY:
REPENTANCE AND TRUST IN GOD

Fourth Luminous Mystery:
TRANSFIGURATION

And as He was praying, the appearance of His countenance was altered and His raiment became dazzling white. And a voice came out of the cloud saying, "This is My Son, My chosen; listen to Him!" (Lk 9:29, 35).

Our Father, 10 Hail Marys, Glory Be, etc.

FRUIT OF THE MYSTERY:
DESIRE FOR HOLINESS

Fifth Luminous Mystery:
INSTITUTION OF THE EUCHARIST

And He took bread, and when He had given thanks He broke it and gave it to them, saying, "This is My body which is given for you." ... And likewise the cup after supper, saying, "This cup which is poured out for you is the new covenant in My blood" (Lk 22:19-20).

Our Father, 10 Hail Marys, Glory Be, etc.

FRUIT OF THE MYSTERY: *ADORATION*

∼ *The Sorrowful Mysteries* ∼

First Sorrowful Mystery:
THE AGONY IN THE GARDEN

In His anguish, He prayed with all the greater intensity, and His sweat became like drops of blood falling to the ground. Then He rose from prayer and came to His disciples, only to find them asleep, exhausted with grief (Lk 22:44-45).

Our Father, 10 Hail Marys, Glory Be, etc.

FRUIT OF THE MYSTERY:
SORROW FOR SIN

Second Sorrowful Mystery:
THE SCOURGING AT THE PILLAR

Pilate's next move was to take Jesus and have Him scourged (Jn 19:1).

Our Father, 10 Hail Marys, Glory Be, etc.

FRUIT OF THE MYSTERY: *PURITY*

Third Sorrowful Mystery:
CROWNING WITH THORNS

They stripped off His clothes and wrapped Him in a scarlet military cloak. Weaving a crown out of thorns they fixed it on His head, and stuck a reed in His right hand (Mt 27:28-29).

Our Father, 10 Hail Marys, Glory Be, etc.

FRUIT OF THE MYSTERY: *COURAGE*

Fourth Sorrowful Mystery:
CARRYING OF THE CROSS

...[C]arrying the cross by Himself, He went out to what is called the Place of the Skull (in Hebrew, Golgotha) (Jn 19:17).

Our Father, 10 Hail Marys, Glory Be, etc.

FRUIT OF THE MYSTERY: *PATIENCE*

Fifth Sorrowful Mystery:
THE CRUCIFIXION

Jesus uttered a loud cry and said, "Father, into Your hands I commend My spirit." After He said this, He expired (Lk 23:46).

Our Father, 10 Hail Marys, Glory Bc, etc.

FRUIT OF THE MYSTERY: *PERSEVERANCE*

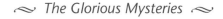

∿ The Glorious Mysteries ∿

First Glorious Mystery:
THE RESURRECTION

You need not be amazed! You are looking for Jesus of Nazareth, the one who was crucified. He has been raised up; He is not here. See the place where they laid Him" (Mk 16:6).

Our Father, 10 Hail Marys, Glory Be, etc.

FRUIT OF THE MYSTERY: *FAITH*

Second Glorious Mystery:
THE ASCENSION

Then, after speaking to them, the Lord Jesus was taken up into heaven and took His seat at God's right hand (Mk 16:19).

Our Father, 10 Hail Marys, Glory Be, etc.

FRUIT OF THE MYSTERY: *HOPE*

Third Glorious Mystery:
DESCENT OF THE HOLY SPIRIT

All were filled with the Holy Spirit. They began to express themselves in foreign tongues and make bold proclamation as the Spirit prompted them (Acts 2:4).

Our Father, 10 Hail Marys, Glory Be, etc.

FRUIT OF THE MYSTERY: *LOVE OF GOD*

Fourth Glorious Mystery:
THE ASSUMPTION

You are the glory of Jerusalem ... you are the splendid boast of our people ... God is pleased with what you have wrought. May you be blessed by the Lord almighty forever and ever (Jth 15:9-10).

Our Father, 10 Hail Marys, Glory Be, etc

FRUIT OF THE MYSTERY:
GRACE OF A HAPPY DEATH

Fifth Glorious Mystery:
THE CORONATION

A great sign appeared in the sky, a woman clothed with the sun, with the moon under her feet, and on her head a crown of twelve stars (Rev 12:1).

Our Father, 10 Hail Marys, Glory Be, etc

FRUIT OF THE MYSTERY:
TRUST IN MARY'S INTERCESSION

Scapulars

Scapulars are Sacramentals

Scapulars fall under the general category of "sacramentals." So, before we take a look at what scapulars are, let's first review what sacramentals are.

The *Catechism of the Catholic Church* teaches that "[Sacramentals] are sacred signs (or actions) which bear a certain resemblance to the sacraments, and by means of which spiritual effects are signified and obtained through the prayers of the Church."[137] More specifically, sacramentals are objects (water, oil, salt, crucifixes, scapulars, medals, etc.) blessed by a bishop, priest, or deacon, or they're actions (blessings, laying on of hands) that help dispose us to receive grace. They "work" by turning our hearts and minds to God when we use them with faith.

Sacramentals are not Sacraments. They don't impart sacramental graces like the Sacraments do. Neither are sacramentals magical: The blessing imparted on an object, such as a scapular, doesn't give it special, mystical powers. But God often grants our petitions for special graces when we use blessed objects with faith.

Scapulars in General

The term "scapular" comes from the Latin word *scapulae*, which means "shoulders." There are two main categories of scapulars: those worn by consecrated religious as part of their habit and those worn by the faithful as a form of devotion. The former consist of a long piece of cloth that usually hangs from the shoulders and reaches down to the knees. The latter, devotional scapular, is much smaller, consisting of two small pieces of cloth joined by thin straps or ribbons, and it usually represents some kind of association with the religious community that wears the scapular. So, for instance, the "brown scapular" is related to the Carmelite Order, whose consecrated members wear a brown habit.

The blue scapular is somewhat unique. This is because none of the religious communities associated with it, for instance, the Conceptionist Nuns, Theatine Fathers, and Marian Fathers of the Immaculate Conception, wear blue habits. Rather, they wear the blue scapular — in its smaller devotional form — underneath their regular religious garb. This blue, "hidden scapular," as it's been called, does not signify membership in any religious community; rather, it signifies a special devotion to Mary and her Immaculate Conception.

There are many different kinds of scapulars: black, brown, blue, red, green, and white. However, because our space here is limited, we're going to treat just two of them: the brown and blue scapulars.

The Brown Scapular

The brown scapular, also known as the Scapular of Our Lady of Mount Carmel, is the most popular devotional scapular. Its popularity stems in large part from the famous apparition of Mary to St. Simon Stock, an English Carmelite, who lived during the mid-thirteenth century.

In the apparition, Mary reportedly held in her hands the brown habit of the Carmelite Order, offered it to St. Simon, and said, "This will be for you and for all Carmelites the privilege, that he who dies in this habit will be saved." The key words are these: "he who dies *in this habit* will be saved." In other words, the promise of Our Lady most likely meant that a faithful Carmelite religious who keeps his vows and lives according to the constitutions of his order, of which his religious garb is a symbol, will die in the state of grace. This promise does not seem so extraordinary when one considers that a faithful Carmelite religious is bound by his vows and constitutions to live a life of renunciation, dedication to prayer, and love of God and neighbor.

Eventually, the Carmelite Order, which consisted of a First Order (priests and friars) and a Second Order (nuns), expanded to include a Third Order of laity, who commit themselves to living out certain norms of Carmelite spirituality. It is widely believed that the promise made by Mary to St. Simon applies also to the members of the Third Order, insofar as these dedicated laity remain faithful to their commitment to prayer and good works, a commitment signified by the devotional scapular that they wear.

Separate from its use by the Third Orders, the brown scapular is also worn by members of the Confraternity of the Brown Scapular. A confraternity is a group of people united by a common profession or purpose, and it is typically a religious group joined by a common spirituality and cooperation in certain good works. The scapular community members strive for the perfection of charity according to the spirit of the Carmelite Order and thereby participate in its spiritual benefits, such as the promise of Our Lady to St. Simon regarding Carmelites.

It should be noted that one can be enrolled in the rite of the brown scapular without joining a confraternity. In 1996, in a statement approved by the Congregation for Divine Worship and the Discipline of the Sacraments, the Church declared that whoever receives the brown scapular becomes a member of the Carmelite Order and pledges oneself to live its spirituality in accordance with one's state in life.

So, all Carmelites are free to believe in the promise made by Our Lady to St. Simon regarding them. However, they need to strive to be faithful to the demands of charity and the way of perfection. In other words, the brown scapular is not a good-luck charm or superstitious "free pass to heaven." Rather, it is a sign of a serious commitment to live an ardent Christian life under the patronage and protection of Our Lady of Mt. Carmel, whose powerful intercession sees to it that her true sons and daughters will be saved.

The Blue Scapular

There's a tradition in the Church that our Lord appeared to Venerable Ursula Benincasa (1547-1618), founder of the Order of Theatine nuns, who helped popularize the practice of wearing the blue scapular of the Immaculate Conception. It is believed that Jesus came to her and promised great favors for her Order, and she asked that he grant those same graces to those who wear the blue scapular in honor of the Immaculate

Conception. She said Jesus granted her request, and she began to distribute the scapulars. A group of wealthy girls who had given up the materialism of the world to live for Our Lord were the first to wear it, because they wanted to wear something to honor the Blessed Virgin Mary in a special way. In 1671, Pope Clement approved a blessing and investiture ceremony for the blue scapular.

The blue scapular symbolizes one's love and devotion to Our Lady and is a sign of trust in her intercession and care. It should also signify a desire on the part of the one who wears it to live as Our Lady did, free of sin and in union with Jesus Christ.

The Congregation of Marian Fathers of the Immaculate Conception began wearing the blue scapular shortly after their founding by Blessed Stanislaus Papczynski (1631-1701). Venerable Casimir Wyszynski (1700-1755), also a member of the Marian Fathers, first approached the Theatine Fathers in 1733 and asked for permission to bless and invest the faithful in the blue scapular, since they were the ones who officially propagated the devotion at the time. In 1734, the Marians officially adopted the use of the blue scapular and promoted it.

Much later, in 1992, the Marians requested and were granted by the Theatine Fathers perpetual permission to bless and confer the scapular. A plenary indulgence given at the hour of death is offered to those who die wearing the scapular, and the permission authorizes the Marians to delegate other priests or deacons to bless and confer the blue scapular. Thus, the Marians have been promoting the wearing of the blue scapular as a means of devotion to Our Lady for more than three centuries.

To obtain more information about joining the Confraternity of the Immaculate Conception of the B.V.M., investiture in the blue scapular, the ensuing duties and spiritual benefits, and information about the scapular itself, please send an e-mail to our Confraternity coordinator (confraternity@marian.org) or fill out our online form at www.marian.org/confraternity. You may also call the toll-free number 1-800-462-7426 (for U.S. and Canada only) to order blue scapulars and the booklet on the blue scapular (please mention its code EBS).

Miraculous Medal

Like the scapular, the miraculous medal is a sacramental. It originates from an apparition of Mary to St. Catherine Labouré, a French nun, living in Paris. The specific apparition that has to do with the miraculous medal occurred on November 27, 1830.

In that vision of November 27, St. Catherine saw Mary standing on a half-globe with a serpent crushed beneath her feet and her hands bejeweled with rings, holding a small golden globe with a cross on it. Bright light shown from some of the jewels on her fingers. Suddenly, the small, golden globe disappeared from Mary's hands, and she opened her arms outward. The light from the jewels extended out from her hands, and a semi-circle frame appeared around and over her with an inscription in gold: "O Mary, conceived without sin, pray for us who have recourse to thee."

The vision seemed to rotate, and on the reverse side, Catherine saw the letter "M" with a cross on it and surrounded by twelve stars. The cross stood on a horizontal bar. Under the "M" were two hearts engulfed in flames, one encircled in thorns and the other pierced by a sword.

Mary then told Catherine, "Have a medal struck upon this model. Those who wear it will receive great graces, especially if they wear it around the neck."

Mary explained the meaning of the medal to Catherine as follows: Mary is Queen of heaven and earth. She crushes Satan, who is helpless before her, under her foot (see Gen 3:15). Her arms are open, and the many rays of light are graces that she obtains for those who request them. The dark jewels, the ones that are not full of light, represent the graces that are available but that people don't receive because they don't ask for them.

The inscription, "O Mary, conceived without sin, pray for us who have recourse to thee," refers to Mary's Immaculate Conception, which means that from the first moment of her conception she was free from all stain of original sin.

On the back of the medal, the twelve stars represent the twelve Apostles, who represent the whole Church, which surrounds Mary. The "M" is for Mary, and the cross is the Cross of Christ, the symbol of our redemption. The horizontal bar represents the earth. The placement of the cross and the bar on and in the letter "M" shows Mary's participation in the Cross of Christ and her involvement in our world. The two hearts are those of Jesus and Mary, burning with love for us all.

With the Church's approval, the first "Medals of the Immaculate Conception" were made in 1832, and almost immediately, reports of miraculous cures began to spring up, so much so that the medal became known as the "miraculous medal."

Since the time of the apparitions, millions of medals have been distributed around the world, especially by people like Blessed Mother Teresa of Calcutta. It's reported that her Missionaries of Charity currently distribute 1.8 million medals per year.

The miraculous medal received liturgical approbation (special recognition and approval for public prayer) at the direction of Aloisi Cardinal Masella, Prefect of the Sacred Congregation of Rites, in 1895. It's one of only three sacramentals in the Church to be so liturgically honored, sharing this distinction with the Rosary and the brown scapular.

Far from being a good luck charm or superstition, powerful conversions have taken place through Mary's intercession and the use of the miraculous medal.

One of the most famous conversions happened to Alphonse Ratisbonne, a Jewish atheist, on January 20, 1842. He despised the Church and the Catholic faith, especially since his older brother, Theodor, converted to Catholicism and became a Catholic priest. On a dare from a Catholic friend, Baron de Bussieres, Ratisbonne began to wear the miraculous medal and to recite the *Memorare* prayer to prove the fruitlessness of what he thought were just the ridiculous superstitions of the Catholic religion.

On January 20th, Ratisbonne accompanied Baron de Bussieres into a church, what is now the Basilica of St. Andrea delle Fratte in Rome, where the Baron had some business to attend to. When the Baron returned to him, he found Ratisbonne weeping and kissing his medal saying, "I saw her! I saw her!"

Ratisbonne later recounted what happened in his diary:

I had only been in the church a moment when I was suddenly seized with an indescribable agitation of mind. I looked up and found that the rest of the building had disappeared. One single chapel seemed to have gathered all the light and concentrated it in itself. In the midst of this radiance I saw someone standing on the altar, a lofty shining figure, all majesty and sweetness, the Virgin Mary just as she looks on this medal. Some irresistible force drew me towards her. She motioned to me to kneel down and when I did so, she seemed to approve. Though she never said a word, I understood her perfectly.[138]

This encounter with Mary so profoundly affected Ratisbonne that he converted to Catholicism and was ordained a priest in 1847. He later moved to the Holy Land with his brother Theodor and founded a congregation of sisters — the Congregation of Our Lady of Sion — to pray for the conversion of the Jews.

An image of Mary as she appeared to Ratisbonne was painted a few months after the apparition and then hung above the altar in the church where Ratisbonne saw her. Later, another devotee of Mary and the miraculous medal, St. Maximilian Kolbe, celebrated his first Mass in the same church in Rome, before the same painting. Apparently, in January of 1917, while he was still a seminarian in Rome, Kolbe had heard a talk on the conversion of Ratisbonne. He continued to meditate on Mary's intercession for this non-believer, for nine months.

In October of the same year, Kolbe began the Militia Immaculata (MI) with six other Franciscans. These young men consecrated their lives totally and unconditionally to Mary for the sake of their own sanctification and the conversion of souls. All members of the MI now wear the miraculous medal as a sign of their total consecration to Mary and distribute it so that Mary may work wonders of grace in the lives of others.

Of the miraculous medal, Kolbe stated:

Even though a person be the worst sort, if only he agrees to wear the medal, give it to him ... and then pray for him, and at the proper moment strive to bring him closer to his Immaculate Mother, so that he have recourse to her in all difficulties and temptation.[139]

Wearing the miraculous medal is a discreet, simple, and effective way to express one's devotion and consecration to Mary, and it disposes us to receive God's grace through her powerful intercession.

Chaplet of the 10 Evangelical Virtues

Introduction

According to St. Louis de Montfort, a key part of living out one's consecration is to imitate Mary's virtues. Yet, in order to imitate her virtues, we need to know them well. We get to know them well by praying the Chaplet of the 10 Evangelical Virtues, which identifies and fosters meditation on 10 virtues of Mary that are taken from the Gospels and that were composed by St. Joan of Valois (d. 1505).

How to Pray the Chaplet

To pray the chaplet, one needs 10 beads of a Rosary or a 10-bead chaplet. Begin with the Sign of the Cross followed by one Our Father. Then, on the 10 beads, pray 10 Hail Marys but with the following addition: After saying "Holy Mary, Mother of God..." insert one of the following virtues:

1. most pure
2. most prudent
3. most humble
4. most faithful
5. most devout
6. most obedient
7. most poor
8. most patient
9. most merciful
10. most sorrowful

After the 10 Hail Marys, pray the Glory Be and then say:

In your Conception, O Virgin Mary, you were Immaculate. Pray for us to the Father whose Son, Jesus, you brought forth into the world.

Conclude with the following prayer:

Father, You prepared the Virgin Mary to be the worthy mother of Your Son. You let her share beforehand in the salvation Christ would bring by His death, and kept her sinless from the first moment of her conception. Help us by her prayers to live in Your presence without sin. We ask this in the name of Jesus the Lord. Amen.

May the Virgin Mary's Immaculate Conception, be our health and our protection.

Optional Petitions

The following petitions, divided according to Mary's virtues, are not actually part of the Chaplet of the 10 Evangelical Virtues. However, bringing these petitions before the Mother of God can help us pray the chaplet more effectively.

The First Virtue: Purity

Mary, you are most pure, both in body and soul. Help me to protect my bodily purity through custody of my eyes and by avoiding anything that would lead to lust. Help me to dress and act modestly, protecting my dignity and recognizing the dignity of others as well.

Let my intentions be pure. Help me to strive to do everything for Jesus, without selfish motives or agendas.

The Second Virtue: Prudence

Virgin most prudent, you pondered in your heart all that God spoke to you throughout your life. You recognized and reflected on all that God was asking of you. Please help me to develop the same attitude of pondering. Help me to reflect on all that God is doing in my life and through the people around me, so I may respond to him with generosity.

The Third Virtue: Humility

Most humble Mother, God lavished on you the extraordinary grace of the Immaculate Conception not on account of your merits, but because it delighted him to do so. Teach me to accept with joy all the graces that God gives me each day, knowing that I don't deserve them.

The Fourth Virtue: Faith

Mary, you are most faithful. You accepted all that God asked of you. So great was your willingness to follow him and place everything in his hands. I worry, faithful Mother, about many things: my life, my family, my job, my future, the future of the country. Teach me to have faith in God. Teach me to place my trust in him as you did, surrendering all things to his holy will.

The Fifth Virtue: Devotion

Most devout Mother and model of prayer, teach me how to pray. Join my little prayers to yours and make them even more pleasing to God. Teach me, most of all, to receive Jesus mindfully in the Eucharist. Help me to talk with him, love him, and listen to him.

The Sixth Virtue: Obedience

Mary, through your loving obedience to the will of God, you brought into the world its Savior. I am often torn between doing my will and doing God's will. Help me to surrender my stubborn will, even if it sometimes seems like I have no hope of changing. Help me also to love the will of God, even when it's difficult to accept.

Seventh Virtue: Poverty

Most poor Mother, your poverty was both physical and spiritual. You had only simple things and yet you saw everything as a gift from God. My possessions can sometimes possess me, and I forget that they, too, are gifts from God insofar as they bring him glory. Help me to rid myself of any attachments to my possessions that distract me from loving God. Also help me to be ever thankful for all the material and spiritual blessings that God gives me.

The Eighth Virtue: Patience

Mary, model of patience, you endured all things with the greatest patience. Here, Mary, I sometimes struggle. When things don't go my way immediately, I can become impatient and sometimes even angry. Teach me to bear trials and burdens in God's time and not according to my own time. Transform my moments of waiting, even in small things like slow traffic or a line at the bank, into moments of peaceful prayer.

The Ninth Virtue: Mercy

Great Mother of Mercy, you brought forth Jesus Christ, who is Divine Mercy Incarnate. You also continually intercede for all of your children here on earth. Teach me how to ask Jesus for mercy and then how to be merciful to others.

The Tenth Virtue: Sorrow for Sin

Most sorrowful Mother, your wounded and pierced heart reminds me of the reality of sin and how much it hurts you when we turn our backs on God. Your love for us is also a source of sorrow in that you are with us as we suffer. Teach me to have true contrition for my sins. Teach me also to turn to you when the trials and sufferings of life seem overwhelming.

Chaplet of the Seven Sorrows of Mary

Introduction

Devotion to the Seven Sorrows of Mary goes back to the Middle Ages and has been promoted by the Servite Order. When Mary appeared to visionaries in Kibeho, Rwanda, she requested that it be recited. The Seven Sorrows are based on Scriptural events in the lives of Jesus and Mary that reveal Mary's sufferings.

The Chaplet of the Seven Sorrows of Mary is prayed on special chaplet beads that are divided into seven sets of seven and has three concluding beads. Each set of seven begins with an Our Father followed by seven Hail Marys. At the end, on the three remaining beads of the chaplet, three Hail Marys are said in honor of the Tears of Our Sorrowful Mother. While reciting the prayers, one meditates on the following.

The First Sorrow — The Prophecy

The prophecy of holy Simeon, who told Our Sorrowful Mother of the bitter Passion and death of Jesus:

> Now there was a man in Jerusalem named Simeon, and this man was righteous and devout, looking for the consolation of Israel, and the Holy Spirit was upon him. And it had been revealed to him by the Holy Spirit that he should not see death before he had seen the Lord's Christ. And inspired by the Spirit he came into the temple; and when the parents brought in the child Jesus, to do for him according to the custom of the law, he took him up in his arms and blessed God and said, Lord, now lettest thou thy servant depart in peace, according to thy word; for mine eyes have seen thy salvation which thou hast prepared in the presence of all the peoples, a light for revelation to the Gentiles and for glory to thy people Israel. And his father and his mother marveled at what was said about him; and Simeon blessed them and said to Mary his mother, "Behold, this child is set for the

fall and rising of many in Israel, and for a sign that is spoken against and a sword will pierce through your own soul also, that the thoughts of many hearts may be revealed" (Lk 2:25-35).

Our Father and Seven Hail Marys.

The Second Sorrow — The Flight

Our Sorrowful Mother is forced to flee into Egypt to save her beloved Son from the death decreed by Herod:

Now when they had departed, behold, an angel of the Lord appeared to Joseph in a dream and said, "Rise, take the child and his mother, and flee to Egypt, and remain there until I tell you; for Herod is about to search for the child, to destroy him." And he rose and took the child and his mother by night, and departed to Egypt, and remained there until the death of Herod. This was to fulfill what the Lord had spoken by the prophet, "Out of Egypt have I called my son" (Mt 2:13-15).

Our Father and Seven Hail Marys.

The Third Sorrow — The Loss

Our Sorrowful Mother is separated from Jesus for three long days when he remains in Jerusalem without her knowing it:

And when the feast was ended, as they were returning, the boy Jesus stayed behind in Jerusalem. His parents did not know it, but supposing him to be in the company they went a day's journey, and they sought him among their kinsfolk and acquaintances; and when they did not find him, they returned to Jerusalem, seeking him. After three days they found him in the temple, sitting among the teachers, listening to them, and asking them questions; and all who heard him were amazed at his understanding and his answers. And when they saw him they were astonished; and his mother said to him, "Son, why have you treated us so? Behold, your father and I have been looking for you anxiously." And he said to them, "How is it that you sought me? Did you not know that I must be in my Father's house?" And they did not understand the saying that he had spoken to them. And he went down with them and came to Nazareth, and was obedient to them; and his mother kept all these things in her heart (Lk 2:43-51).

Our Father and Seven Hail Marys.

The Fourth Sorrow — The Meeting

Our Sorrowful Mother meets Jesus on the road to Calvary and sees him fall under the cruel weight of the cross:

And there followed him a great multitude of the people, and of women who bewailed and lamented him. But Jesus turning to them said, "Daughters of Jerusalem, do not weep for me, but weep for yourselves and for your children. For behold, the days are coming when they will say, 'Blessed are the barren, and the wombs that never bore, and the breast that never gave suck!' Then they will begin to say to the mountains, 'Fall on us'; and to the hills, 'Cover us.' For if they do this when the wood is green, what will happen when it is dry?" (Lk 23:27-30).

Our Father and Seven Hail Marys.

The Fifth Sorrow — Jesus Dies

Our Sorrowful Mother watches Jesus die on the Cross:

So the soldiers did this. But standing by the cross of Jesus were his mother, and his mother's sister, Mary the wife of Clopas, and Mary Magdalene. When Jesus saw his mother, and the disciple whom he loved standing near, he said to his mother, "Woman, behold, your son." Then he said to the disciple, "Behold, your mother." And from that hour the disciple took her to his own home. After this Jesus, knowing that all was now finished, said (to fulfill the scripture), "I thirst." A bowl full of vinegar stood there; so they put a sponge full of the vinegar on hyssop and held it to his mouth. When Jesus had received the vinegar, he said, "It is finished"; and he bowed his head and gave up his spirit (Jn 19:25-30).

Our Father and Seven Hail Marys.

The Sixth Sorrow — Mary Receives Jesus

Our Sorrowful Mother receives the dead body of Jesus in her arms:

Since it was the day of Preparation, in order to prevent the bodies from remaining on the cross on the Sabbath (for that Sabbath was a high day), the Jews asked Pilate that their legs might be broken, and that they might be taken away. So the soldiers came and broke the legs of the first, and of the other who had been crucified with him; but when they came to Jesus and saw that he was already dead, they did not break his legs. But one of the soldiers pierced his side with a spear, and at once there came out blood and water. He who saw it has borne witness — his testimony is true, and he knows that he tells the truth — that you also may believe. For these things took place that the Scripture might be fulfilled, "Not a bone of him shall be broken." And again another scripture says, "They shall look on him whom they have pierced" (Jn 19:31-37).

Our Father and Seven Hail Marys.

The Seventh Sorrow — The Burial

Our Sorrowful Mother sees Jesus placed in the sacred tomb:

There were also women looking on from afar, among whom were Mary Magdalene, and Mary the mother of James the younger and of Joses and Salome, who, when he was in Galilee, followed him, and ministered to him; and also other women who came up with him to Jerusalem. And when evening had come, since it was the day of Preparation, that is, the day before the Sabbath, Joseph of Arimathea, a respected member of the council, who himself was also looking for the kingdom of God, took courage and went to Pilate, and asked for the body of Jesus. And Pilate wondered if he were already dead; and summoning the centurion, he asked him if he were already dead. And when he learned from the centurion that he was dead, he granted the body to Joseph. And he bought a linen shroud, and laid him in a tomb which had been hewn out of the rock; and he rolled a stone against the door of the tomb. Mary Magdalene and Mary the mother of Joses saw where he was laid (Mk 15:40-47).

Our Father and Seven Hail Marys.

Conclusion

Three Hail Marys are said in honor of the Tears of Our Sorrowful Mother.

Endnotes

[1] *True Devotion to Mary*, trans. Frederick W. Faber (Rockford, IL: TAN Books, 1985), n. 55. See also nn. 152-168.

[2] English translation of the *Catechism of the Catholic Church: Modifications from the Editio Typica* copyright © 1997, United States Catholic Conference, Inc. — Libreria Editrice Vaticana, n. 2701ff.

[3] Address to the de Montfort Fathers, cited in *True Devotion*, p. vi.

[4] Ibid., n. 114.

[5] Ibid.

[6] Ibid., n. 47.

[7] Ibid., n. 177.

[8] Mary's specially appointed task in the work of salvation does not in any way detract from Christ as the one who perfectly completes this work in himself. That Christ shares this work with Mary (and all of us) shows forth its greatness. Thus, the *Catechism* (citing the Second Vatican Council document, *Lumen Gentium* 60, 62) states:

> Mary's function as mother of men in no way obscures or diminishes [the] unique mediation of Christ, but rather shows its power. But the Blessed Virgin's salutary influence on men … flows forth from the superabundance of the merits of Christ, rests on his mediation, depends entirely on it, and draws all its power from it.
>
> … No creature could ever be counted along with the Incarnate Word and Redeemer; but just as the priesthood of Christ is shared in various ways both by his ministers and the faithful, and as the one goodness of God is radiated in different ways among his creatures, so also the unique mediation of the Redeemer does not exclude but rather gives rise to a manifold cooperation which is but a sharing in this one source (970).

[9] Eddie Doherty, *Wisdom's Fool: A Biography of St. Louis de Montfort* (Bay Shore, NY: Montfort Publications, 1993), p. 31.

[10] The Jansenist heresy was very strict and legalistic. It was fixated on our sinfulness and not mercy. According to the Jansenists, one has to be perfect and clean even to think of approaching Jesus, and one has to earn God's love. They didn't like St. Louis de Montfort because of the way he emphasized the mercy of God, especially as it's given to us through Mary. The Jansenists didn't like to think about the mercy of God. They wanted people always to fear God and only think of his justice.

[11] Battista Cortinovis, SMM, "Saint Louis-Marie Grignon de Montfort," n.d., <http://www.3op.org/stlouis.php> (accessed October 10, 2011).

[12] *True Devotion*, n. 198.

[13] Ibid., n. 52.

[14] Ibid., n. 121.

[15] Ibid., n. 198.

[16] Ibid., n. 147.

[17] See Ibid., n. 132, which reads:

> [I]t is not credible that our parents, friends, and benefactors should suffer from the fact of our being devoted and consecrated without exception to the service of Our Lord and His holy Mother. To think this would be to think unworthily of the goodness and power of Jesus and Mary, who know well how to assist our parents, friends, and benefactors out of our own little spiritual revenue or by other ways.
>
> This practice does not hinder us from praying for others, whether dead or living, although the application of our good works depends on the will of our Blessed Lady. On the contrary, it is this very thing which will lead us to pray with more confidence; just as a rich person who has given all his wealth to his prince in order to honor him the more, would beg the prince all the more confidently to give an alms to one of his friends who should ask for it. It would even be a source of pleasure to the prince to be given an occasion of proving his gratitude toward a person who had stripped himself to clothe him, and impoverished himself to honor him. We must say the same of our Blessed Lord and of Our Lady. They will never let themselves be outdone in gratitude.

[18] *Diary of St. Maria Faustina Kowalska: Divine Mercy in My Soul* (Stockbridge: Marian Press, 1987), n. 605. The passage reads:

> O Holy Trinity, Eternal God, I thank You for allowing me to know the greatness and the various degrees of glory to which souls attain. Oh, what a great difference of depth in the knowledge of God there is between one degree and another! Oh, if people could only know this! O my God, if I were thereby able to attain one more degree, I would gladly suffer all the torments of the martyrs put together. Truly, all those torments seem as nothing to me compared with the glory that is awaiting us for all eternity.

[19] *True Devotion*, n. 144. Also, it's interesting to read n. 28 in this context: "In the Heavens Mary commands the angels and the blessed. As a recompense for her profound humility, God has empowered her and commissioned her to fill with saints the empty thrones from which the apostate angels fell by pride."
[20] Ibid., n. 133.
[21] Ibid., n. 82.
[22] Ibid., n. 154. See also n. 152:

> We do find, it is true, great battles to fight, and great hardships to master; but that good Mother makes herself so present and

so near to her faithful servants, to enlighten them in their darkness and their doubts, to strengthen them in their fears, and to sustain them in their struggles and their difficulties, that in truth this virginal path to find Jesus Christ is a path of roses and honey compared with the other paths.

23 Ibid., n. 155.
24 Ibid., n. 122.
25 Ibid., n. 208.
26 See Ibid., n. 218-219, which reads:

How many devout souls do I see who seek Jesus Christ, some by one way or by one practice, and others by other ways and other practices; and oftentimes, after they have toiled much throughout the night, they say, "We have toiled all night, and have taken nothing! (Lk 5:5). ...

Take notice, if you please, that I say the saints are molded in Mary. There is a great difference between making a figure in relief by blows of a hammer and chisel, and making a figure by throwing it into a mold. Statuaries and sculptors labor much to make figures in the first manner; but to make them in the second manner, they work little and do their work quickly.

27 Ibid., n. 210. See also n. 203:

[Mary] is on the lookout ... for favorable occasions to do [her true children] good, to advance and enrich them. She sees clearly all good and evil, all prosperous and adverse fortunes, the blessings and the cursings ... and then she disposes things from afar that she may exempt her servants from all sorts of evils, and obtain for them all sorts of blessings. ... "She herself takes care of our interests," says a certain saint.

And n. 209:

[Mary] conducts and directs [her devotees] according to the will of her Divine Son. ... She shows them the paths of eternal life. She makes them avoid the dangerous places. ... "If you follow her," says St. Bernard, "you cannot wander from the road." Fear not, therefore, that a true child of Mary can be deceived by the evil one, or fall into any formal heresy. There where the guidance of Mary is, neither the evil spirit with his illusions, nor the heretics with their subtleties, can ever come.

28 Patricia Treece, *A Man for Others: Maximilian Kolbe, Saint of Auschwitz* (Huntington, IN: Our Sunday Visitor, 1982), p. 1.
29 Ibid., p. 9.

[30] Ibid., p. 160.

[31] H.M. Manteau-Bonamy, OP, *Immaculate Conception and the Holy Spirit*, trans. Richard Arnandez, FSC (Libertyville, IL: Franciscan Marytown Press, 1977), p. 2.

[32] Here is the official, infallible declaration by Pope Pius IX, some four years prior to the apparitions at Lourdes:

> The most Blessed Virgin Mary was, from the first moment of her conception, by a singular grace and privilege of almighty God and by virtue of the merits of Jesus Christ, Savior of the human race, preserved immune from all stain of original sin (*Catechism of the Catholic Church*, n. 491).

[33] Manteau-Bonamy, p. 3.

[34] Ibid.

[35] Ibid., pp. 4-5.

[36] See Paul VI's Beatification homily for Maximilian Kolbe on October 17, 1971:

> No one should disapprove if Blessed Maximilian and the Church together with him show such enthusiasm for the formal veneration of the most Blessed Virgin; this enthusiasm will never be too great considering the merits and the advantages we can derive from such veneration, precisely because a mysterious communion unites Mary to Christ, a communion that is documented convincingly in the New Testament. Never let us think of this as "Mariolatry"; we know that the sun will never be dimmed by the light of the moon; and never will the ministry of salvation entrusted to the Church's solicitude in particular be impaired, if the Church is faithful to honor in Mary her most exceptional Daughter, and her spiritual Mother."

[37] *The Book of the Sentences*, St. Thomas Aquinas, I, dist. 14, q. 2 a. 2 as cited in *Immaculate Conception and the Holy Spirit*, p. 38.

[38] Manteau-Bonamy, p. 3.

[39] Ibid., p. 4.

[40] Ibid.

[41] Luigi Faccenda, OFM Conv., *One More Gift*, trans. Father Kolbe Missionaries of the Immaculate (West Covina, CA: Immaculata Press, 1990), pp. 74-75.

[42] Treece, p. 73.

[43] *Aim Higher!: Spiritual and Marian Reflections of St. Maximilian Kolbe*, trans. Dominic Wisz, OFM Conv. (Libertyville, IL: Marytown Press, 2007), p. 15.

[44] Treece, p. 67.

[45] *Aim Higher!*, p. 129.

[46] Ibid., p. 13.
[47] Manteau-Bonamy, p. 43.
[48] Faccenda, pp. 51-52.
[49] Treece, pp. 68-69.
[50] Ibid., p. 66.
[51] *Aim Higher!*, p. 129.
[52] Ibid.
[53] Ibid., pp. 129-130.
[54] Ibid., p. 45.
[55] *Mother Teresa: Come Be My Light: The Private Writings of the "Saint of Calcutta,"* ed. Brian Kolodiejchuk, MC (New York: Doubleday, 2007), p. 14.
[56] Ibid., 48.
[57] Ibid., 67.
[58] Ibid., 68.
[59] Ibid., 41.
[60] Ibid., 149.
[61] Ibid., 214.
[62] Ibid., 216.
[63] *A Life for God: Mother Teresa Treasury*, ed. Lavonne Neff (NY: Harpercollins, 1996), p. 139.
[64] John Paul II's message for Lent 1993 reads:

> Dear brothers and sisters, … . Listen to the voice of Jesus who, tired and thirsty, says to the Samaritan woman at Jacob's well: "Give me a drink" (Jn 4:7). Look upon Jesus nailed to the Cross, dying, and listen to his faint voice: "I thirst" (Jn 19:28). Today, Christ repeats his request and relives the torments of his Passion in the poorest of our brothers and sisters (The Holy See, Message of His Holiness John Paul II for Lent 1993, September 18, 1992, <http://tinyurl.com/JPIIThirstMessage> [accessed August 15, 2011]).

[65] Mother Teresa's letter to the Missionaries of Charity family, 25th March 1993 © 2011 Missionaries of Charity Sisters, c/o Mother Teresa Center. Used with permission.
[66] *Come Be My Light*, p. 99.
[67] Ibid.
[68] Ibid.
[69] Joseph Langford, MC, *Mother Teresa: In the Shadow of Our Lady: Sharing Mother Teresa's Mystical Relationship with Mary* (Huntington, IN: Our Sunday Visitor, 2007), p. 24-25.
[70] Ibid., p. 40.
[71] *Aim Higher!*, p. 13.
[72] See *In the Shadow of Our Lady*, p. 72.
[73] The examination of conscience (also called "examen") should be made sometime toward the end of the day. Most people make it shortly before

going to bed. It's basically a mental review of the previous 16 hours or so of consciousness — thus, some people prefer to call the examination of conscience an examination of consciousness.

To make the examen, first, we should put ourselves in the presence of God. In other words, we should begin with the attitude that the examen is a time of prayer, not just a mental exercise. Devoutly making the Sign of the Cross may be enough to do this.

Next, we just have to remember one word: baker, B-A-K-E-R, baker. Actually, we also have to remember what each letter of this word stands for. Let's start with "B."

B stands for "blessings." According to St. Ignatius, this is the most important of the five points. Here we simply review our day, survey the many blessings God has given us throughout it, and then praise and thank him for these blessings. For instance, maybe we had a great conversation with someone at lunch. During the examen, we might want to reflect on that gift and praise and thank God for it. Of course, we don't have to go through every single blessing of the day. That would take way too much time. The key is to let one's heart roam about and settle on the particular peaks of joy and blessing of the day, what Ignatius calls "consolation." One more thing: We shouldn't forget to thank God for the crosses of the day, which are also blessings.

If we get into the habit of praising and thanking God like this every day during our examen, then we'll begin to better recognize the blessings of our day as they happen, and thus, we'll develop a continual attitude of gratitude. In other words, our praise and thanks won't begin to flow simply when we make our examen — it'll flow all day long. Furthermore, as God sees our efforts to recognize and thank him for his many gifts, he'll send us more and more.

A stands for "Ask." Although we already placed ourselves in the presence of God when we began the examen, here we need to ask for a special grace from the Holy Spirit, the grace to recognize our sins. Without the help of the Holy Spirit, we'll remain blind to our sinfulness. Thus, when we get to this second point, we need to ask the Holy Spirit to help us recognize our sinfulness, which brings us to the next point.

K stands for "Kill." Why "kill"? Because it was our sins that killed and crucified Jesus. During this third point, we look at our sinfulness (weaknesses and attachments, too). So, again, we gaze across the conscious hours of our day. This time, however, we look not for peaks but valleys, what Ignatius calls "desolation." In other words, we pay attention to those times during our day when our hearts dropped. Why might they have dropped? Maybe because of someone else's sin. Maybe someone said something unkind to us. Fine. Did we forgive them? If so, good. If not, well, the examen is a good time to deal with it.

Now, let's keep looking. Here's another time our hearts dropped. It was this afternoon at work, standing by the water cooler. Hmmm. Why did our hearts drop then? Ah, yes (thanks, Holy Spirit), that's when we stuck Bob with a verbal barb. Let's see, anything else? Yes, there's another heart dropper: We didn't accept the traffic jam on our way home as a small sharing in the Cross. We should have been more peaceful about it and offered it up as a prayer for others.

Okay, so after remembering all those heart-dropping moments, we may feel pretty down. Such a feeling may make us want to run away from Jesus. Let's not. When the weight of our sinfulness drags us down, that's the best time to go to Jesus, sinfulness and all — which brings us to the next point.

E stands for "embrace." This is to allow Jesus to embrace us, sinners that we are, with the rays of his merciful love. While praying over this point, it may be helpful to think of the Image of Divine Mercy. I like to imagine the rays of this image embracing me with forgiveness. I also like to remember Jesus' words that it rests his Heart to forgive and that when I go to him with my sinfulness, I give him the joy of being my Savior. I believe that at this point of the examen, we greatly console Jesus when we simply let him embrace us with his merciful love — and of course, we, too, are consoled. I recommend spending some time lingering on this point (in the embrace) before moving on to the next.

R stands for "Resolution." During this last point of the examen, we take what we've learned from the previous points and look ahead to the next day, ready to make resolutions. For instance, having recognized during "K" that we stuck Bob with a verbal barb at the office today, we might resolve that tomorrow morning we'll make it up to him by going to his cubicle, slapping him on the back, and congratulating him on how his football team did earlier this evening. Also, having remembered that we were impatient during the traffic jam today, we can resolve to bite our tongues if the sea of brake lights appears again tomorrow. Finally, because during "B" we realized that God was speaking to us during our lunchtime conversation with Sally, giving light on a certain problem, we can resolve to act on that light by looking up the online article she recommended. (I think we get the idea.)

[74] *Come Be My Light*, p. 31.

[75] Scott Hahn, *A Father Who Keeps His Promises: God's Covenant Love in Scripture* (Ann Arbor, MI: Servant Publications, 1998), p. 26.

[76] Langford, p. 78

[77] The translation used in the Mass for this verse is taken from the Douay-Rheims Bible. In the RSV and other translations, the verse is Psalms 69:20.

[78] *Come Be My Light*, p. 260-261.

[79] Ibid., p. 321.

[80] Ibid., p. 171.

[81] Ibid., p. 233.

[82] George Weigel, *Witness to Hope: The Biography of Pope John Paul II* (New York: HarperCollins, 1999), p. 413.

[83] In his book, *Gift and Mystery: On the Fiftieth Anniversary of My Priestly Ordination* (New York: Doubleday, 1996), John Paul explains the meaning of the phrase "*Totus Tuus*," which is his papal motto. He says the phrase comes from St. Louis de Montfort and that the words are "an abbreviation of a more complete form of entrustment to the Mother of God, which runs

like this: *Totus Tuus ego sum et omnia mea Tue sunt. Accipio Te in mea Omnia. Praebe mimic or Tuum, Maria"* (p. 30).
[84] *Lumen Gentium*, n. 61.
[85] Ibid., nn. 61-62.
[86] *Redemptoris Mater*, n. 39.
[87] Ibid., n. 20.
[88] Ibid.
[89] Ibid., nn. 21-22.
[90] Ibid., n. 18.
[91] Ibid., n. 23.
[92] Ibid.
[93] Ibid., n. 39.
[94] Ibid., n. 24.
[95] Ibid., n. 44.
[96] Ibid.
[97] Ibid., n. 45.
[98] Ibid.
[99] Ibid., n. 46.
[100] These were John Paul's words during a greeting to English-speaking pilgrims at his first general audience in Rome after returning from this trip to Fatima in May, 1982. To read the text, see footnote 103.
[101] Act of Entrustment, Pope John Paul II, May 13, 1982, n. 9. See also his use of these words during his Act of Entrustment of May 13, 1984, which are cited in the reflection for Day 22.
[102] Homily of Pope John Paul II in Fatima, Portugal on May 13, 1982, n. 8.
[103] This phrase comes from John Paul's greeting to English-speaking pilgrims at his first general audience in Rome after his return from Fatima (May, 1982), cited by Arthur Calkins in *Totus Tuus: John Paul II's Program of Marian Consecration and Entrustment* (Libertyville, IL: Academy of the Immaculate, 1992), p. 177. On that occasion, the Pope said:

> Last week I myself went on pilgrimage to Portugal, especially to Fatima, in order to give thanks that the mercy of God and the protection of the Mother of Christ had saved my life last year. The message of Fatima is a call to conversion and penance, the first and most basic call of the Gospel. Today it is more urgent than ever, when evil is threatening us through errors based on denial of God. The message of Fatima puts us on our guard. It also invites us to approach anew the Fountain of Mercy by an act of consecration. Mary wishes us to draw near to it: each one of us, each nation, and the whole world.

[104] Homily, 1982, n. 8.
[105] Ibid., n. 9.
[106] Act of Entrustment, May 13, 1982, n. 2.
[107] Ibid.
[108] Ibid.

[109] *Theotokos: Woman, Mother, Disciple* (Boston: Pauline Books and Media, 2000), p. 38.
[110] *True Devotion to Mary*, n. 36.
[111] Ibid., 20.
[112] Regarding the point that Mary does not take us away from Jesus but leads us to him, de Montfort writes:

> Mary was created only for God, and it is unthinkable that she should reserve even one soul for herself. On the contrary she leads every soul straight to God and to union with him. Mary is the wonderful echo of God. The more a person joins himself to her, the more effectively she unites him to God. When we say "Mary," she re-echoes "God" ("The Secret of Mary" *in God Alone: The Collected Writings of St. Louis Marie de Montfort* [Bay Shore, NY: Montfort Publications, 1995], p. 268).

[113] *Aim Higher!*, p. 43.
[114] Treece, p. 66.
[115] *The Kolbe Reader*, ed. Anselm W. Romb, OFM Conv. (Libertyville, IL: Franciscan Marytown Press, 1987), p. 96.
[116] Langford, p. 72.
[117] Msgr. Arthur Burton Calkins, "The Theology of the Alliance of the Hearts of Jesus and Mary," n.d., <http://www.christendom-awake.org/pages/calkins/alliance.htm> (accessed October 1, 2011).
[118] Pope Pius XII, *Audience on the Occasion of Louis de Montfort's Canonization* (July 21, 1947). Emphasis added.
[119] "The Secret of Mary," nn. 43-44.
[120] Ibid., nn. 45-46.
[121] *The Kolbe Reader*, p. 99.
[122] Ibid., p. 112.
[123] Ibid., p. 128.
[124] It is a doctrine of the Catholic Church that we are called to participate in Jesus' redeeming action in the world. In other words, as we read in the introduction, Jesus doesn't just redeem us and then expect us to kick back and relax. On the contrary, he includes us in the work of redemption, and an important part of this work is our suffering. Specifically, Jesus invites us to unite our suffering with his in order to save souls: He invites us to be "co-redeemers," redeemers "with him," though in an entirely subordinate way to himself.

We approach the mystery of "co-redemption" when we reflect on some puzzling words of St. Paul: "I rejoice in my sufferings for your sake, and in my flesh I complete what is lacking in the suffering of Christ for the sake of his body, the Church ..." (Col 1:24). How can St. Paul write that there's something "lacking" in the suffering of Christ? Jesus' suffering is objectively enough to save everyone, and the graces of his suffering are available to all. In this sense, there's absolutely nothing lacking in his suffering. Yet there's a kind of "lack" in Christ's suffering in the sense that not everyone subjectively accepts his grace and mercy. Moreover, there's also a lack in his suffering when people don't fully accept his grace and mercy, that is, when they do so halfheartedly and with reservations and conditions. It's precisely in such situations where people reject or don't fully accept God's grace that our sufferings and prayers can come in to "complete what is lacking."

So, Jesus didn't come to take away our suffering — he came to transform it. With Christ, suffering is no longer a meaningless burden. Yes, we still suffer, but now, if we're in the state of grace and unite our sufferings to those of Jesus, they have salvific value; they save souls; they give life to others. "That's great," you might be saying, "but how do I unite my sufferings to Christ?" It's simple. Give them to Mary. Mary was most united to Jesus in his suffering on the Cross, and when we give her our sufferings, she herself unites them to those of Jesus and to her own. Yes, even to *her own*.

Mary's sufferings at the foot of the Cross were greater than the sufferings of any other creature, and she offered them with the greatest love. To better understand her suffering and love, reflect on the following: If you were to ask any mother who has a child that is suffering terribly if she would rather switch places with her child, of course, she would immediately respond that she would switch places without hestitation. Such is the love of a mother. Now, just think that if you took all the love in the heart of every mother in the cosmos and put it into one heart, that love wouldn't equal the love that Mary has for Jesus. Also, consider that her son is the most loveable of all. Now consider that he was brutally beaten, insulted, and slowly killed right in front of her. Imagine her suffering? We cannot. Hers truly is the greatest suffering of any creature. Her heart was truly pierced with a sword. She truly was "spiritually crucified" with Jesus through love, through her perfectly compassionate love.

Now, if I can be a "co-redeemer" with Christ by offering up my own puny sufferings to him, then obviously Mary is also a co-redeemer. In fact, because of her extraordinary suffering with Christ, she deserves a special title, which many Popes have given her: "Co-Redemptrix." This title doesn't mean that she's equal to Christ but rather that she suffered with him in an extraordinary and subordinate way. (The prefix "co" doesn't mean "equal to" but "with.") This title is in recognition that she, more than anyone else, cooperated in Christ's work of redemption. And just as she has a special role in the Body of Christ of giving birth to "other Christs" through her prayers, so she has a special role in uniting us to Jesus' saving death. It's her job to help us unite our sufferings with Jesus, to bring us, in our suffering, face to face with the love of the Heart of Jesus crucified. Moreover, she augments the merits of our sufferings with her unfathomable merits, merits that she won through her painful union with Christ on the Cross as his loving mother.

How good it is to be consecrated to Mary! She helps us not to waste our sufferings. She unites them, with her own, to the Cross of Christ. Thus, she makes our sufferings superabundantly meaningful and meritorious for the life of the world.

[125] Ibid., p. 120.
[126] Ibid., p. 145.
[127] Ibid., p. 15.
[128] "The Secret of Mary," n. 48.
[129] Joseph Pieper, *Only the Lover Sings: Art and Contemplation* (San Francisco: Ignatius Press, 1990), p. 66.
[130] Here's a list of Marian Feasts by date (those in blue are on US calendar):

1 January – Solemnity of Mary, Mother of God
8 January – Our Lady of Prompt Succor
23 January – Espousal of the Virgin Mary
24 January – Madonna del Pianto (Our Lady of Tears)
2 February – Purification of Mary
11 February – Optional Memorial of Our Lady of Lourdes
25 March – Solemnity of the Annunciation
26 April – Our Lady of Good Counsel
13 May – Optional Memorial of Our Lady of Fatima
24 May – Our Lady Help of Christians, Europe
31 May – Feast of the Visitation of Mary, Our Lady of All Nations
9 June – Our Lady Virgin Mother of Grace
27 June – Our Lady of Perpetual Help
16 July – Optional Memorial of Our Lady of Mount Carmel
17 July – Humility of the Blessed Virgin Mary
2 August – Our Lady of the Angels
5 August – Dedication of the Basilica of Saint Mary Major in Rome
13 August – Our Lady, Refuge of Sinners
15 August – Solemnity of Mary's Assumption into Heaven
21 August – Our Lady of Knock, Ireland
22 August – Memorial of the Queenship of Mary
26 August – Our Lady of Czestochowa
29 August – Our Lady of Good Health
8 September – Feast of the Nativity of Mary
12 September – Most Holy Name of Mary
15 September – Memorial of Our Lady of Sorrows
19 September – Our Lady of La Salette
22 September – Our Lady Queen of Peace
24 September – Our Lady of Walsingham
1 October – Holy Protection of the Mother of God
7 October – Memorial of Our Lady of the Most Holy Rosary
8 October – Our Lady of Good Remedy
11 October – Maternity of the Blessed Virgin Mary
16 November – Our Lady of Mercy (of the Dawn Gate)
21 November – Memorial of the Presentation of Mary
27 November – Our Lady of the Miraculous Medal
29 November – Our Lady of Beauraing
3 December – Our Lady of Victories
8 December – Solemnity of the Immaculate Conception
12 December – Feast of Our Lady of Guadalupe

Here is a list of moveable Marian feast days, in other words, feast days that change their date from year to year:

Memorial of the Immaculate Heart of Mary – Saturday after
    Corpus Christi
Our Lady, Queen of the Apostles – Saturday after Ascension
Our Lady, Health of the Sick – Saturday before the last
    Sunday in August
Our Lady of Consolation – Saturday after the Feast of
    Saint Augustine
Mary, Mother of Divine Providence – Saturday before 3rd
    Sunday of November

There are currently four types of "feasts." From most to least important they are as follows: solemnity, feast, memorial, and optional memorial. The term "feast" has two meanings: First, it means a feast proper (the second most important type of celebration). Second, it's used generically to mean a celebration regardless of rank.

The four most important Marian feasts (solemnities) in the calendar are as follows: Mary's Divine Motherhood (Jan. 1), her Immaculate Conception (Dec. 8), her Assumption (Aug. 15), and the Annunciation (March 25). Of these four feasts, the feasts of Mary's Divine Motherhood, Immaculate Conception, and Assumption are holy days of obligation under the Code of Canon Law: Canon 1246 (1). With the prior approval of the Apostolic See, the Bishop's Conference can suppress certain holy days of obligation or transfer them to a Sunday.

[131] The pious practice of Five First Saturdays began after Our Lady's apparitions at Fatima. In the July apparition in 1917, Mary said to Lucia, "I shall come to ask ... that on the First Saturday of every month, Communions of reparation be made in atonement for the sins of the world."

It wasn't until December 10, 1925, when Our Blessed Mother again appeared to Lucia (this time at Pentevedra, Spain, where Lucia had been sent to learn to read and write from the Dorothean Sisters) that she completed her request for the Five First Saturdays.

She told Lucia:

See, my daughter, my Heart encircled by thorns with which ungrateful men pierce it at every moment by their blasphemies and ingratitude. Do you, at least, strive to console me. Tell them that I promise to assist at the hour of death with the graces necessary for salvation all those who, in order to make reparation to me, on the First Saturday of five successive months, go to confession, receive Holy Communion, say five decades of the Rosary, and keep me company for a quarter of an hour, meditating on the fifteen mysteries of the Rosary.

The practice of the First Saturdays consists of the following elements performed with the intention of reparation and for five consecutive months:

- Confession (before or after the First Saturday — so long as the person receives Holy Communion in a state of grace),
- Holy Communion received on the First Saturday,
- The Holy Rosary, five decades recited sometime during the day,
- Meditating for 15 minutes on the mysteries of the Rosary (one or more).

[132] *The Book of Her Life* (Vol. 1) in *The Collected Works of St. Teresa of Avila* (3 Vols.), trans. Kieran Kavanaugh, OCD, and Otilio Rodriguez, OCD (Washington: Institute of Carmelite Studies, 1976-1987), 4, 9.

[133] See the Vatican website (search *Rosarium Virginis Mariae*) or find this pdf version at http://www.scborromeo.org/docs/apos_ltr_rosary.pdf

[134] *Rosarium Virginis Mariae*, n. 15.

[135] *Catechism*, n. 2725ff.

[136] Ibid., n. 1085. Emphasis in original.

[137] Ibid., n. 1667.

[138] Roy. H. Schoeman, "Salvation is From the Jews," n.d., <http://www.salvationisfromthejews.com/alljews.html#ratisbonne> (accessed September 14, 2011).

[139] Father Kolbe Missionaries of the Immaculata, "The Miraculous Medal," n.d., http://tinyurl.com/KolbeMiraculousMedal (accessed September 14, 2011).

Cheat Sheet

STARTING DATE CHART

START OF THE 33 DAYS	MARIAN FEAST	CONSECRATION/ FEAST DAY
January 9	Our Lady of Lourdes	February 11
February 20*	The Annunciation	March 25
April 10	Our Lady of Fatima	May 13
April 28	The Visitation	May 31
Varies	Immaculate Heart	Saturday after Corpus Christi
June 13	Our Lady of Mt. Carmel	July 16
July 13	The Assumption	August 15
July 20	Queenship of Mary	August 22
August 6	Nativity of Mary	September 8
August 10	Holy Name of Mary	September 12
August 13	Our Lady of Sorrows	September 15
September 4	Our Lady of the Rosary	October 7
October 19	Presentation of Mary	November 21
November 5	Immaculate Conception	December 8
November 9	Our Lady of Guadalupe	December 12
November 29	Mother of God	January 1
December 31	Presentation of the Lord	February 2

* During a leap year, when February has 29 days, the starting date is February 21.

DAILY PRAYERS

Start daily prayers with, *Come, Holy Spirit, living in Mary.*

WEEK ONE: St. Louis de Montfort

Day 1: *Help me to make this retreat with generosity and zeal.*
Day 2: *Prepare me to give myself fully to living out this true and solid devotion.*
Day 3: *Give me the grace to reject Satan and follow Christ more closely.*
Day 4: *Help me to give myself entirely to Jesus through Mary.*
Day 5: *Help me be generous in giving all I have to Mary.*
Day 6: *Help me to give great glory to God by giving all I have to Mary.*
Day 7: *Help me to praise you for such a quick, easy, and secure path to holiness!*

WEEK TWO: St. Maximilian Kolbe

Day 8: *Make me pure in body and spirit and help me to die to myself.*
Day 9: *Unveil for me the meaning of the Immaculate Conception.*
Day 10: *Unveil for me the meaning of the Immaculate Conception.*
Day 11: *Renew the face of the earth, so that all creation may return to God.*
Day 12: *Unite my will to the will of the Immaculata, which is one with your will.*
Day 13: *Prepare me to be a fit instrument in the hands of the Immaculata.*
Day 14: *Prepare me to give all to the Immaculata for the sake of the kingdom.*

WEEK THREE: Blessed Mother Teresa

Day 15: *Help me to find the love of the Heart of Jesus hidden in the darkness.*

Day 16: *Help me listen to Jesus' thirst.*

Day 17: *Bring me face to face with the love in the Heart of Jesus crucified.*

Day 18: *Keep me in her most pure and Immaculate Heart.*

Day 19: *Help me to recognize and ponder in my heart all the good you do for me.*

Day 20: *Help me to ardently make a Covenant of Consecration with Mary.*

Day 21: *Help me to "be the one" to console Jesus with Mary.*

WEEK FOUR: Blessed John Paul II

Day 22: *Have mercy on us and on the whole world!*

Day 23: *Fill my heart with praise to God for giving Mary as my spiritual mother.*

Day 24: *Help me to be faithful to heart-pondering prayer, as was Mary.*

Day 25: *Remind me to ask for Mary's powerful intercession in my times of need.*

Day 26: *Thank you for the gift of my loving Mother, Mary.*

Day 27: *Prepare me to entrust myself completely to Mary so she can bring me closer to Christ.*

Day 28: *Draw me in, with, and through Mary to the Fountain of Love and Mercy.*

FINAL FIVE DAYS: Synthesis and Review

Day 29: *Spend the day pondering de Montfort's Marian teaching as it is summarized by these three words: PASSION, BAPTISM, and GIFT.*

Day 30: *Spend the day pondering Kolbe's Marian teaching as it is summarized by these three words: MYSTERY, MILITIA, and LOVE.*

Day 31: *Spend the day pondering Teresa's Marian teaching as it is summarized by these three words: THIRST, HEART, and COVENANT.*

Day 32: *Spend the day pondering John Paul's Marian teaching as it is summarized by these three words: MOTHER, ENTRUST-ACRATION, and MERCY.*

Day 33:

MORNING GLORY CONSECRATION PRAYER

I, _____, a repentant sinner, renew and ratify today in your hands, O Immaculate Mother, the vows of my Baptism. I renounce Satan and resolve to follow Jesus Christ even more closely than before.

Mary, I give you my heart. Please set it on fire with love for Jesus. Make it always attentive to his burning thirst for love and for souls. Keep my heart in your most pure Heart that I may love Jesus and the members of his Body with your own perfect love.

Mary, I entrust myself totally to you: my body and soul, my goods, both interior and exterior, and even the value of all my good actions. Please make of me, of all that I am and have, whatever most pleases you. Let me be a fit instrument in your immaculate and merciful hands for bringing the greatest possible glory to God. If I fall, please lead me back to Jesus. Wash me in the blood and water that flow from his pierced side, and help me never to lose my trust in this fountain of love and mercy.

With you, O Immaculate Mother — you who always do the will of God — I unite myself to the perfect consecration of Jesus as he offers himself in the Spirit to the Father for the life of the world. Amen.

For a summary of the Church's teaching on Mary visit:
http://marian.org/mary/catechism.php

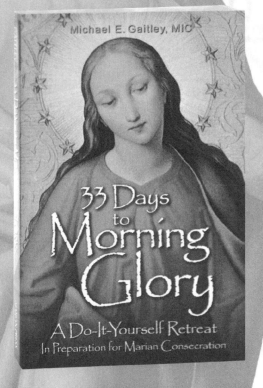

Here's How the Group
Retreat Works:

1. Gather a group.
Better yet, gather several groups of six to twelve people who want to consecrate themselves to Jesus through Mary.

2. Find a place to meet.
Ideally, this would be at a parish with the permission of the pastor, but your group can also meet at someone's home.

3. Read, Ponder, Meet ("RPM")
Get revved up! and...

- *Read...*
  Read the daily meditation in the retreat book, *33 Days to Morning Glory.*

    - *Ponder...*
      Ponder the daily meditation with the help of the *Retreat Companion.*

        - *Meet...*
          Meet with your group for weekly prayer, discussion, and to watch the accompanying talks on DVD.

Here's What You'll Need:
(Details to follow.)

1. The Retreat Book

Everyone will need
one of these.

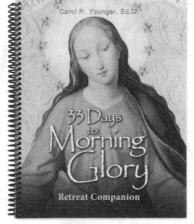

2. The *Retreat Companion*

Everyone will need one
of these, too.

3. DVD Set

Just the Retreat Coordinator will need this.

How to Get What You'll Need:

1. Choose a Retreat Coordinator

The Retreat Coordinator is the person who will organize and run the group retreat.

(The responsibilities of the Retreat Coordinator are explained in the video tutorial and free, downloadable guide available at our website, AllHeartsAfire.org.)

2. Order Your Retreat Materials

Typically, the Retreat Coordinator orders all the materials for the group retreat at the same time to save on shipping. But anyone can order their own materials. To place your order, call toll-free or visit:

1-866-767-3155
LighthouseCatholicMedia.org/HAPP

3. Have Product Codes Ready

The materials mentioned on the previous page come in packets or kits. *The Retreat Coordinators get the kits; the Retreat Participants get the packets.* There are four product codes to choose from for the retreat materials. Have them handy when you order:

PARTICIPANT PACKET (*with* retreat book) = LH_PTPKWB

PARTICIPANT PACKET (*without* retreat book*) = LH_PTPK

COORDINATOR KIT (*with* retreat book) = LH_COKTWB

COORDINATOR KIT (*without* retreat book*) = LH_COKT

---

* If you already have the retreat book, *33 Days to Morning Glory: A Do-It Yourself Retreat in Preparation for Marian Consecration,* you can order your packet or kit without it.

The Participant Packet
and Coordinator Kit

PARTICIPANT PACKET INCLUDES:

- *33 Days to Morning Glory Retreat Companion*
- Prayer Card with Consecration Prayer
- *Collection of Daily Prayers,* a greeting-card-sized compilation of the daily prayers for each week.
- Rosary (colors will vary)
- Pamphlet on How to Pray the Rosary
- Miraculous Medal
- 8 ½ x 11 full-color Consecration Day Certificate

COORDINATOR KIT INCLUDES:

- 33 Days to Morning Glory Participant Packet

  – *33 Days to Morning Glory Retreat Companion*

  – Prayer Card with Consecration Prayer

  – *Collection of Daily Prayers,* a greeting-card-sized compilation of the daily prayers for each week.

  – Rosary (colors will vary)

  – Pamphlet on How to Pray the Rosary

  – Miraculous Medal

  – 8 ½ x 11 full-color Consecration Day Certificate

- *33 Days to Morning Glory: Retreat Talks by Fr. Michael Gaitley, MIC* (DVD set: six sessions, approximately 36-min each)
- *Retreat Coordinator's Guide*

*Both the Participant Packet and Coordinator Kit are available with or without the Retreat Book, *33 Days to Morning Glory*. (See product code information on oppostite page.) Photos above include the Retreat Book.

Up Next...

Continue your small-group experience with the next group retreat based on the best-selling book, *Consoling the Heart of Jesus.*

For more information about the Consoling the Heart of Jesus Group Retreat and other programs, please visit:

LighthouseCatholicMedia.org/HAPP

The 33 Days to Morning Glory and Consoling the Heart of Jesus group retreats are brought to you by Hearts Afire: Parish-based Programs from the Marian Fathers of the Immaculate Conception (HAPP®), and Marian Press, the Marian's publishing apostolate (see ads on following pages).